UTOPIA

Also available in the same series:

Beyond Good and Evil: The Philosophy Classic
by Friedrich Nietzsche (ISBN: 978-0-857-08848-2)

Meditations: The Philosophy Classic
by Marcus Aurelius (ISBN 978-0-857-08846-8)

On the Origin of Species: The Science Classic
by Charles Darwin (ISBN: 978-0-857-08847-5)

Tao Te Ching: The Ancient Classic
by Lao Tzu (ISBN: 978-0-857-08311-1)

The Art of War: The Ancient Classic
by Sun Tzu (ISBN: 978-0-857-08009-7)

The Game of Life and How to Play It: The Self-Help Classic
by Florence Scovel Shinn (ISBN: 978-0-857-08840-6)

The Interpretation of Dreams: The Psychology Classic
by Sigmund Freud (ISBN: 978-0-857-08844-4)

The Prince: The Original Classic
by Niccolo Machiavelli (ISBN: 978-0-857-08078-3)

The Republic: The Influential Classic
by Plato (ISBN: 978-0-857-08313-5)

The Science of Getting Rich: The Original Classic
by Wallace Wattles (ISBN: 978-0-857-08008-0)

The Wealth of Nations: The Economics Classic
by Adam Smith (ISBN: 978-0-857-08077-6)

Think and Grow Rich: The Original Classic
by Napoleon Hill (ISBN: 978-1-906-46559-9)

The Prophet: The Spiritual Classic
by Kahlil Gibran (ISBN: 978–0–857–08855-0)

The Communist Manifesto: The Political Classic
by Karl Marx and Friedrich Engels (ISBN: 978–0–857–08876–5)

A Room of One's Own: The Feminist Classic
by Virginia Woolf (978-0-857-08882-6)

Letters from a Stoic: The Ancient Classic
by Seneca (978-1-119-75135-9)

UTOPIA
The Influential Classic

THOMAS MORE

With an Introduction by
NIALL KISHTAINY

CAPSTONE
A Wiley Brand

This edition first published 2021

Introduction copyright © Niall Kishtainy 2021

This Capstone Classics edition of Thomas More's *Utopia* is based on the Gilbert Burnet translation.

The Gutenberg Project: http://www.gutenberg.org/cache/epub/2130/pg2130.txt.

The Gutenberg version is drawn from *Sir Thomas More's Utopia. Burnet's Translation.* Edited by Henry Morley. London, Cassell & Company, 1889.

The prefatory letters and other materials are sourced from Open Utopia, edited by Stephen Duncombe, under a creative commons licence: https://theopenutopia.org/home/.

Registered office
John Wiley & Sons Ltd, The Atrium, Southern Gate, Chichester, West Sussex, PO19 8SQ, United Kingdom

For details of our global editorial offices, for customer services and for information about how to apply for permission to reuse the copyright material in this book please see our website at www.wiley.com.

A catalogue record for this book is available from the Library of Congress.

A catalogue record for this book is available from the British Library.

ISBN 9781119754381 (Cloth)
ISBN 9780857088956 (epdf)
ISBN 9780857088932 (epub)

Cover design: Wiley

Set in 12/16pt, NewBaskervilleStd by SPi Global, Chennai, India.

10 9 8 7 6 5 4 3 2 1

Printed and bound by CPI Group (UK) Ltd, Croydon, CR0 4YY

CONTENTS

Map of Utopia by Abraham Ortelius (1527–1598) circa 1595

AN INTRODUCTION

BY NIALL KISHTAINY

In 1516, a book written in Latin was published with the invented word 'utopia' in its title: *Concerning the Best State of a Commonwealth, and the New Island of Utopia*. It described an imaginary place, a good society located somewhere in the New World. The book contained a map of a distant island and a translation of a curious alphabet purportedly used by the islanders. *Utopia*, as the book became known, was Thomas More's most famous work and one of the most celebrated of Renaissance Europe.

More was not the first to imagine an alternative civilization: Plato did so in his *Republic*, but More created a literary form that inquired into social conditions using vivid storytelling rather than theory. A poem at the start of the book hails *Utopia's* vision as surpassing Plato's because it goes beyond the abstract: 'For what Plato's pen has plotted briefly, In naked words, as in a glass, The same have I performed fully, With laws, with men, and treasure fitly.'

More was born in London in 1478 and spent most of his life in the city. He became a lawyer of great distinction and held a variety of posts before becoming secretary to Henry VIII and in 1529, Lord Chancellor.

Today he is remembered for his opposition to the king's divorce from Catherine of Aragon, which led to the break from Rome of the English church.

For refusing to bow to the king's wishes, More was executed in 1535. He became a legendary figure in British history, to many a fault-less Catholic martyr. In our secular times, we prefer to view him as a hero of conscience who defended individual belief in the face of tyranny. With *Utopia*, he is seen as a social prophet whose vision for a better world continues to inspire. More was canonized by the Catholic Church in 1935. In 2000 Pope John Paul II declared him the patron saint of politicians.

THE WRITING OF *UTOPIA*

In 1515, More was sent to Bruges as part of a diplomatic mission charged with settling a trade dispute between England and Flanders. During a lull in the talks, More visited Antwerp where he stayed with the town clerk, Peter Giles, with whom he developed a close friendship. Antwerp was then Europe's leading commercial city, and Giles one of its prominent officials and a highly learned man. The time in Antwerp had a stimulating effect on More. While at leisure there he conceived and began to write *Utopia*.

There appears, therefore, to have been an element of serendipity in the composition of *Utopia*, but in fact the ideas in it had been brewing in More's mind for years. By the time of the Bruges mission, More was a busy lawyer, and was Undersheriff of London. He had become a Member of Parliament and had negotiated on behalf of the Mercers' trading company, which represented wool and cloth merchants. These activities would have made More well aware of the social problems facing Tudor England as its commercial economy grew and traditional ways of life were displaced.

Steeped in theological and classical learning, More had become one of the most brilliant scholars of his day. When a young man, he had caught the attention of England's men of letters by delivering a se-ries of lectures on *The City of God*, the vast work written at the end of the Roman Empire by the early Christian father, St Augustine of Hippo. Augustine's central idea was that of two cities that exist within human society: the worldly city of temporal desire and sin and the godly city of peace and fulfilment. Augustine was a major influence on More's spiritual development, and the idea of the two cities applied to social questions most likely fuelled the thinking that went into *Utopia*. A few years earlier, More had begun writing *A History of Richard III*, an account of the king whose defeat by Henry Tudor at Bosworth Field ushered in the Tudor reign. Richard's notoriety came in part from More's unflattering portrait of him in this work. Through Richard's story, the book deals with questions of tyranny and of sound kingship.

Utopia, then, was written by a man of considerable intellectual and practical credentials. More knew the law inside out, moved in the highest scholarly and court circles, and in his early works had already begun thinking about the pressing social and political problems of the day. Authors of the utopian tracts of the eighteenth and nineteenth centuries aimed their works at a wide audience, hoping that their ideas would be adopted in practical programmes of reform. *Utopia*'s sixteenth-century audience was much narrower: the book was written for the elite Latin-speaking scholars of Europe rather than the bakers and butchers of More's daily life in London.

THE ISLAND OF UTOPIA

Utopia takes the form of a traveller's tale told by a seafarer who once chanced upon the island of Utopia. During a series of dialogues with various interlocutors the explorer tells of life on the happy island and makes scathing critiques of English society. The story starts with real events and with More himself, who begins by telling of his mission to Flanders and his journey to Antwerp.

The fiction starts when More recalls one day stepping into the street after Mass and seeing Peter Giles talking to a sun-beaten mariner. Giles tells him that the man, Raphael Hythloday, is a traveller with amazing tales of far-off lands. The men retire to a garden and Raphael tells More and Giles about his travels generally, his views on

ix

the state of contemporary Europe, and about the distant nation of Utopia.

In Raphael's description of Utopia, we encounter a society that in some of its surface features resembles England. For example, like London, Utopia's capital city of Amaurot lies on a hill by a tidal river with a stone bridge over it. But at a deeper level Utopia is an inversion of the societies of England and Europe. In Utopia property is held in common and there is no money. Whenever a family needs food or clothes, the head of the household goes to the city warehouse and takes what is required. The Utopians are a disciplined, frugal people devoted to the higher pleasures of conversation and learning. They have no reason to take more goods than they need, having no desire to flaunt their possessions. Their sturdy houses have no locks on the doors and are exchanged every ten years by lot.

One of the most memorable Utopian customs, used to show the Utopians' rejection of opulence, is the making of chamber pots out of gold and the public shaming of wrongdoers by placing gold crowns on their heads. Pearls and diamonds are given to the children for playthings; they discard the baubles as they grow up.

In Utopia everyone works in the fields or at handicrafts, unlike in Europe where societies are dragged down by the wasteful extravagance and idleness of noblemen and their retainers. Because all lend a hand and there is no need for luxuries, the Utopian working day is short and there is plenty of time left over to engage in learning and contemplation. There are only a few laws, simple enough for everyone to understand, and no lawyers. The Utopians come together for their meals, during which a morally improving text is read out and discussed. After dinner, the people play music or converse in their gardens.

Utopia ranges over many questions including: war (the Utopians hate the pursuit of military glory that Europe's princes lust after); the qualities of priests (the Utopians' priests are few in number and truly pious, unlike those in Europe); the functioning of politics (aimed at avoiding tyranny); and marriage customs (divorce is allowed in special circumstances and infidelity is punished). But the communal principle of *Utopia* is the big theme that encompasses all of these, and at two places in the book Raphael pauses his travelogue to deliver tirades about the impossibility of justice in societies based on private property. More and Giles raise objections, arguing that without private property society could not function because people would not bother to work. Raphael is undaunted. The rich will always exploit the poor, he says, through private fraud and by capturing the law. Policies to mitigate these defects will never have much of an effect while there is still private property. Raphael hails Utopia as the best commonwealth because with everything held in common everyone is guaranteed their subsistence. The abolition of property and money ends fraud, murder, disorder, and anxiety. What would stop the adoption of utopian arrangements, then? Human pride, which measures fortune by the ill-fortune of others.

UTOPIA AND THE REAL WORLD

Utopia is divided into two books. Book One begins with the fictional More's meeting with Raphael, then leads into a series of dialogues between Raphael, More, and Giles. Raphael's recollections of conversations that he had while visiting England introduce a number of other characters. These first conversations are not about Utopia directly, the topic of the island appearing almost as an aside.

On hearing Raphael's descriptions of the different societies that he saw during his travels, Giles says that Raphael should become an adviser to a king, where his knowledge could be put to good use. But Raphael says that courts are places of flattery and rigid convention where the ideas of visionary philosophers are misunderstood and ignored. Much of the rest of Book One is a tug of war between Raphael on one side and More and Giles on the other, the latter two pressing the case for public service on the unshakeable Raphael.

During this discussion Raphael reports a conversation that he had in England that shows the futility of serving kings. At a dinner, a lawyer had praised the harsh punishment given to thieves. Raphael replied that such punishments were pointless and wrong because in an unjust society the poor had to steal to survive. Then comes a famous passage in which Raphael identifies another cause of theft: sheep, which in their grazing swallow up people and whole villages. Raphael is condemning the enclosure of land then underway in England in which agricultural common lands were fenced off and turned over to the raising of sheep for the lucrative wool trade. As a result, farming communities were thrown off the fields and into poverty. The lawyer rejects Raphael's argument for less severe punishments, claiming that they would threaten public order. The other guests agree with the lawyer, but when the distinguished master of the house says that Raphael's argument may have merit, they quickly do an about-turn. This, says Raphael, illustrates his point that courts are filled with sycophants who simply parrot what they think their masters want to hear.

How do Books One and Two relate to each other? Book Two in narrative terms is the less complex, consisting mainly of Raphael's description of Utopia. More actually wrote this book first. Book One is a swirl of voices, in turn quizzical, curious, and disputatious, that together probe questions of practical politics and statecraft seemingly removed from the grand social vision of Book Two. It is telling that More began Book Two while on a sojourn away from his usual London life and turned to Book One when back in the city and immersed again in his legal and official duties. Book One frames Book Two by exploring how radical solutions can be made into reality. Can we hope for utopia in a world of imperfect politics?

This question has lain at the heart of utopian debates ever since, echoed in the argument between Raphael, More, and Giles about where visionaries should employ their talents. To maintain their ideological integrity, many utopians have since followed Raphael in wishing to stay aloof from the grubby, compromised world of politics.

At the end of Book One, the fictional More sets out a middle way. Raphael's social visions are speculative and abstract and hard to fathom for most people, says More. In the court of a king they would fall on deaf ears if expounded without taking proper account of the context. The problem is that such abstract philosophy lacks sensitivity to its setting and its audience – to the stage on which political life is played out. More instead advocates a philosophy that is tailored to the audience, one pursued by the wise visionary who realizes that though politics is imperfect there is no reason to stay aloof from it. Through tact and judgement one may manage things 'so that, if you are not able to make them go well, they may be as little ill as possible'.

MORE'S CAREER DILEMMA

As More worked on Utopia, he was himself facing the question of

Hans Holbein's *Sir Thomas More* (1527), Frick Collection

whether to get more closely involved with political life by becoming a royal official. From a young age, More had moved in circles of privilege and influence and seemed destined to hold high office. But he was also a person of deep spiritual yearning. At the beginning of his legal career in the early years of the sixteenth century, More undertook intense theological study. One result was his lectures on St Augustine. He also attached himself to the Charterhouse, a Carthusian monastery just outside London's city walls, where he followed a regimen of prayer and fasting.

An important part of More's later image is that during these years he was hankering after the life of a scholar-monk, but was being sought out as an official by the king. It was said he was reluctant to agree to royal service, wanting to serve God and not the worldly intrigues of the court. His friend, the great Dutch scholar Desiderius Erasmus, claimed that More had to be 'dragged' to court.

It is true that More disliked the pomp and ostentation of court culture. But on his return from Bruges he was a regular visitor to court, always making sure to pay his respects to the Lord Chancellor, Thomas Wolsey. It is possible that the perception of More as a reluctant courtier is part of the busy legend-making pursued by himself and by his friends and early biographers. In all likelihood, More was simply seeking the middle way that his fictional alter ego in *Utopia* recommended: to be an intellectually independent but practical courtier who, despite the compromises of political life, sought at least to do some good and to reduce harm. Thus, in 1518, More became a member of the King's Council and soon became the king's secretary. He acted as a go-between between Henry and Wolsey, who, until his fall in 1529, would be England's most powerful official.

A UTOPIAN IN TUDOR ENGLAND

It was an auspicious time for a man of More's interests and background to enter royal service. The question of Henry's divorce that would later lead to Wolsey's fall and to More's execution had yet to dominate English politics. The civil wars known as the Wars of the Roses had ended in the late fifteenth century when More was still a boy. The Tudors had come to power, putting the English nation state on a more stable footing.

With European explorers discovering and plundering new lands, international trade routes were opening up and England was becoming an important trading power and London a major commercial hub. When Henry VIII took the throne in 1509, More wrote verses hailing the dawn of a new era of prosperity and justice. Henry was himself a scholar, and a new breed of learned courtiers began to emerge, like More drawn from middling social ranks and trained in the law.

More and many of his friends at court were connected to the Christian humanist scholarship that had originated in Renaissance Italy and spread to Northern Europe during the fifteenth century. Its exponents returned to original Greek and Latin texts, revived classical rhetoric that would give new ideas practical as well as intellectual potency, and rejected the abstract logical methods of medieval scholastic philosophy. More and other humanist scholars believed that the renovation of literary scholarship would promote human virtue, a purer form of Christianity, and a better society. Erasmus and More were leading lights of this movement and forged a famous friendship and intellectual partnership. Helped through publication by Giles and Erasmus, *Utopia* was one of the most famous literary creations of this new cultural setting.

Thomas Wolsey epitomized the opulence and worldly ambition of the court that More deplored, but he was a champion of the new learning and was promoting policies that would find parallels in *Utopia*. Wolsey attempted to reform the inefficient and sclerotic English legal system, which had long disadvantaged the poor. In 1517, he established a commission on the enclosure of common land, then illegal, and attempted to prosecute those undertaking such practices.

When More became Lord Chancellor in 1529, he continued Wolsey's legal efforts to make the law swifter and more accessible to the poor. More may even have considered dedicating *Utopia* to Wolsey, and it has been conjectured that the book inspired Wolsey to set up his enclosure inquiry. It is hard to draw precise connections between Wolsey's and More's actual policies and the new forms of society set out in *Utopia*. However, the echoes of one in the other are another reason for believing that More might have been less conflicted about entering royal service than many of his biographers have assumed.

Another echo of *Utopia* in More's life is found in the reputation of his family as having been especially learned and virtuous. More had four children by his first wife, Jane Colt, who died in her early twenties; his second wife, the well-off Alice Middleton, acted as stepmother and stayed with him until his death. The family followed a routine of prayer and study and all were encouraged in cultural pursuits. More's children were carefully educated in the classics and religion and his favourite, Margaret, became one of the most learned women in England. At mealtimes, a religious text would be read out and discussed. Erasmus called the household a Platonic Academy devoted to study and spiritual cultivation. Visiting scholars would come to stay, courtiers pass through, and sometimes even the king would drop in for dinner. More's admirers have thought of his home as a little humanist Utopia, a place of scholarship, Christian virtue, and public duty.

MORE'S INTENTION IN *UTOPIA*

The subtitle of More's opus – *A Truly Golden Little Book, No Less Beneficial than Entertaining* – raises the central critical problem of *Utopia* that its readers have been arguing about ever since: what did More intend? Is the book meant as a piece of literary entertainment or as social instruction? If we are meant to take its social arguments seriously, then which of the opposing characters' views are we meant to believe? Is the real More instructing us about how to take our own societies closer to perfection, or is he saying that this is a futile endeavour? Who speaks for the real More: the fictional More and Giles, the sceptics, or Raphael, the arch-radical?

This sense of ambiguity runs through the text, which is full of word play and paradox, starting with the word *utopia* itself. It is a Greek-derived neologism of More's that could mean 'good place' (*eu-topia*) or 'no place' (*ou-topia*). The river that flows through Amaurot is called Anyder or 'waterless' and the governor of Utopia is named

Ademus, 'without a people'. Even the shape and dimensions of the island described by Raphael turn out to be mathematically impossible. Raphael Hythloday bears as his first name that of the archangel who came to heal, yet the second part of his name means 'peddler of nonsense'. Finally, More was fond of punning the Latin version of his name, *Morus*, the Greek for 'fool'. It raises the question: if Raphael peddles nonsense, then why does the fictional More oppose him with the objections of a halfwit?

This slipperiness is reinforced by the story's basis in real events and people as well as the inclusion in the text of a map, alphabet, and prefatory letters. In one of these letters, More apologizes to Giles for taking so long to finish the book. He admits that he was at first worried about the challenge of arranging the material and expressing it elegantly, but then realized that all he really had to do was to 'write plainly the matter as I heard it spoken'. He tells Giles that now he has got to the end of the writing he finds that a few details have slipped his mind, such as the width of the bridge spanning the Anyder. Was it five hundred or three hundred yards long? Would Giles mind getting in touch with Raphael and asking him to settle the matter – and while he is at it, clear up a crucial point which More is embarrassed not to have clarified at the time, that is, where in the New World is Utopia actually located? In another letter, Giles says that during their conversations, Raphael did mention the location of the island but, as he did so, someone nearby coughed loudly, drowning out the crucial words. Giles promises to find Raphael and ask him, though there are rumours that he died on his way home or that he returned to Utopia.

This sense of literary play remains even in that part of the text in which Raphael drily catalogues the customs of the Utopians, even without interjections from More and Giles. Some of these seem designed to puzzle and confound. There are slaves in Utopia (people are not born slaves but are made into them as punishment) and the death penalty is used for certain offences. Utopia is a society of strict control and surveillance: the Utopians can only travel with official permission and discussions about public policy outside the senate are punishable by death. The Utopians foment plots in enemy nations and hire assassins to kill enemy leaders.

Here it must be remembered that More wrote before the advent of modern liberalism and individualism, and so to us some of the Utopians' practices look highly objectionable. But they would have looked much less so to a person of the early sixteenth century. What are we to make, though, of the Utopian practice of displaying potential marriage partners naked so that they can inspect each other before deciding to marry – just as one examines a horse before buying it? One modern critic quipped: 'So this is Utopia is it? I beg your pardon; I thought it was hell.'

INTERPRETING *UTOPIA*

Many of the earliest responses to *Utopia* passed over the paradoxical aspects of the text and took what More said at face value. Some of his contemporaries took More's game playing literally. One reader was said to have been so excited by More's description of Utopia that he asked to be sent there in the capacity of Bishop. Even those who did not believe that Utopia was a real place often assumed that More earnestly sought to describe a perfect commonwealth that could be used as a criticism of existing societies and as a means for reforming them.

Later commentators were more sensitive to the various layers of the text, which made More's intentions and real views harder to pin down. One way of dismissing the seriousness of More's social vision has been to identify the views of the real More with the firmest denials of Raphael's arguments by the fictional More. A particularly influential interpretation of *Utopia* from Raymond Chambers in the 1930s downplays its radical content: More's tale is in fact an allegorical lament for the old medieval world of piety and communal life and a rejection of the new one of commerce and individual striving. In this view, More drew on his experience at the Charterhouse to imagine Utopia as a spiritual idyll in the form of an expanded monastery. This place of piety was created by pagans ignorant of Christ and the Bible who, through the exercise of natural reason, created a religion similar to Christianity. Utopia then stands as a criticism of Christian Europe, which has degenerated into corruption and impiety and falls far short of the virtue achieved by the non-Christian Utopians. By this view, More is one of the last great medieval Catholics, a conservative trying to hold back the tide of modernity.

From the nineteenth century, More began to be seen as an early communist, and Raphael as voicing More's true conscience. After the Russian Revolution, Lenin had an obelisk erected in Moscow which celebrated thinkers who promoted the liberation of humankind. Alongside the names of Marx and Engels was that of Thomas More. Socialist and communist thought sets out a path of history from feudalism to capitalism. Contradictions within capitalism blow that system apart, making way for socialism. Socialist champions of More such as Karl Kautsky in the late nineteenth century saw much of this in *Utopia*: the condemnation by Raphael of enclosure is of a piece with Marx's account of the accumulation and dispossession that drive the creation of the capitalist economy. Wealth falls into the hands of a few and creates a landless poor that endures great suffering. When Raphael attacks the harsh punishment of thieves, he voices an important socialist principle: that people's choices are limited by the material conditions that they find themselves in. Their lives, and therefore their actions, can be elevated by improving those conditions.

Yet socialism grew out of a critique of the smoky factory capitalism of the nineteenth century, which pitted a mass proletariat against large capitalists. This was far from the England of More's time, which still retained remnants of a feudal economy. Utopia had a handicraft economy quite different to the industrial one which socialists considered to be the foundation of a future socialist system. Both capitalism and socialism pursue by different means the end of satisfying growing human wants. Utopia, on the other hand, is a disciplined society of ascetics which aims at the restriction of desire. Gains in the efficiency of production are used not to give people more goods or mindless leisure but to allow them more time for study and self-improvement.

Although the content and context of modern socialism are different from those of *Utopia*, More's book shines a light on the negative impacts of the money economy. In championing a communal way of life, it does anticipate the social vision of later socialism. The view of *Utopia* as an elegy for medieval Catholicism has been challenged, but even if we prefer to view More as a forward-looking radical rather than a backward-looking conservative, it reminds us in our secular times not to ignore the religious context of More's work. More revered the monastic way of life when it was carried out with proper discipline, and this is reflected in the high-minded lives of the Utopians.

But Utopia is much more than a monastery writ large: it is a nation with a government, with families in which children are born and raised, and with armies that go to war when they have to. Our final glimpse of the Utopians comes at the end of Book Two when we see them at prayer in their temple. They thank God for placing them in a happy commonwealth, but ask that if their society falls short of perfection, God will show them their error. They promise to try out any new social arrangements that will take them closer to perfection. In their prayer they show the willingness of true radicals, socialist or otherwise, to boldly throw off the past and to discard unprofitable traditions in favour of better ways of life.

More recent interpretations such as those of Elizabeth McCutcheon and Dominic Baker-Smith have emphasized the paradoxical nature of *Utopia*. Anticipating postmodern concerns with multiple perspectives and the subjectivity of truth, *Utopia*'s irony and its play of opposing voices are perhaps its point. More's linguistic ploys unmoor the reader from commonplace social beliefs so that unorthodox ideas can be introduced and explored. Far from proposing a complete utopian blueprint, More tells his story of the good society through a set of shifting perspectives so as to lay bare the promises and pitfalls of the utopian quest. This is arguably the best context within which to deal with the question of who the real More was and with the potentially confounding aspects of Utopian life. Perhaps the real More, himself a complex and highly paradoxical man, is both the fictional More and Raphael.

Utopianism is a dynamic, experimental ,and never-ending method of social inquiry, not one in which perfection can easily be defined and implemented. This sense that the search for utopia has to be an open-ended pursuit that must balance different perspectives is hinted at when Raphael has completed his description of Utopia. The fictional More says that much of what Raphael described 'seemed very absurd'. As Raphael appears to be tired from talking, instead of arguing with him further, More leads him into supper, expressing hope for further opportunities for discussion.

Utopia closes on a note of equivocation from More: 'I cannot perfectly agree to everything he has related. However, there are many things in the commonwealth of Utopia that I rather wish, than hope, to see followed in our governments.'

UNCOVERING MORE THE MAN

In his later career, More was caught up in the turmoil of Reformation politics. His biographical persona has often been moulded by historians according to their religious and political allegiances, making it hard to uncover the 'real' More. The earliest accounts of his life from which we gain many biographical details were written by people close to him. Many were hagiographies aimed at building the case for More's sainthood. They present More as witty, learned, and industrious, a morally spotless man who bravely died for the Catholic Church.

More lost some of his repute in Protestant England. The author of the first English translation of *Utopia*, published after the Reformation, included a rebuke in his introduction, saying that More was a man of 'incomparable wit' and 'profound knowledge' but 'obstinate' in matters of religion 'even to the very death'. More was gradually absolved of his refusal to conform. His anti-clericalism and desire for a purer church were used to rehabilitate him as a Protestant reformer in spirit if not in name.

Twentieth-century historians led by Geoffrey Elton and Richard Marius revised these portrayals of a righteous More to reveal a complex, imperfect figure. One line of attack has been on More's involvement in the detection and punishment of Lutheran heretics when in Henry VIII's service. More's admirers have downplayed his role in these campaigns, but revisionist historians have seized on it as evidence of More being a religious fanatic – drawing a contrast with the earlier humanist More who wrote *Utopia*. One highly critical account by Jasper Ridley claims that if More had lived in the twentieth century he would have been the kind of zealot who in the service of an ideology justifies the death of millions.

Revisionist historians have also returned to the question of why More put aside his apparent aspirations to become a monk for family and official life. Some have argued that he chose to marry out of sheer sexual frustration, and that his decision tormented him for the rest of his life. He would only achieve a resolution of sorts at the end of his days when imprisoned in his cell, living like a monk, praying and writing spiritual tracts. More, who wore a hair shirt under his clothes and whipped himself before the altar, under this less favourable view was a brooding, conflicted man, much less attractive than the earlier picture of him. A version of this darker image appears in the acclaimed 2009 novel *Wolf Hall* by Hilary Mantel, which caused controversy for its less than flattering depiction of More.

These critical views have been a useful corrective to More hagiography, and help to explore the tensions at the heart of More's life and work. Both approaches often go too far though. Balanced assessments try to avoid seeing More as saint or villain and concede that much of the internal motivation for his actions cannot be known.

Despite the scholarly controversies, the popular heroic image of More is still very much alive, most famously in the play by Robert Bolt, *A Man For All Seasons*, which premiered in London in 1960 and was later made into two films. Here More becomes a sort of liberal exemplar, bravely standing up for his conscience in the face of tyranny. Speaking of the religious belief that has brought him into conflict with the king,

Bolt's More says: 'What matters to me is not whether it's true or not, but that I believe it to be true, or rather not that I *believe* it, but that *I* believe it.' This is not the utterance of a devout Catholic of the early sixteenth century. In the modern secular world it is how we understand More and how we make him into an icon for our own times.

THE LEGACY OF *UTOPIA*

With *Utopia*, More began a lineage of utopian thinkers who have used storytelling and social analysis to explore new possibilities for society. Many later utopians wrote social blueprints and plans rather than fantastical tales, but they often cited More's *Utopia* as inspiration. In the late nineteenth century, utopians returned to storytelling. With the New World by then mapped out, it became a less compelling setting for tales of undiscovered perfect societies, so utopian stories often moved readers through time rather than space.

For example, in 1888 the American author Edward Bellamy published *Looking Backward*, which depicted a future America transformed into a technologically advanced socialist utopia. In 1890, the British writer and artist William Morris hailed More's *Utopia* as 'a living work of art' and published his own, *News from Nowhere*, which showed a future London transformed into a quasi-medieval communal idyll.

It is often supposed that after the utopian optimism of the nineteenth century we now live in anti-utopian times. With the horrors of the twentieth century fresh in our historical imaginations, grand utopian visions are often dismissed as at best naive, at worst a first step towards totalitarianism. True believers seek to obliterate all that stands in their way.

With the collapse of communism in the late twentieth century, it became common to believe that there is no alternative to capitalism, that market forces and money are the only viable way of running societies. Utopias like More's, based on a communal way of life, seemed ever less feasible.

Yet it is human nature to yearn for a better life, and the utopian impulse is never very far below the surface. From the Occupy protests following the 2008 financial crisis, through to Extinction Rebellion climate activists, and even the spread of 'mutual aid' organizations during the pandemic, which mobilized communities to assist the most vulnerable, people still seek to create new forms of society. Proposals for a universal basic income, once considered naive utopian fancy, are now taken seriously in policy circles.

Many of these movements oppose 'neoliberal' capitalism, which is based on a belief in market forces, financial capital, and the human as self-interested individual. Inflated property prices, which benefit owners but exclude many from their own cities, are today's version of More's people-eating sheep: profit and the market come before human values and the community. Critics on the Left argue that rising inequality and the enrichment of the 'one percent' mean that social mobility is stalling. These modern complaints echo *Utopia's* Raphael and his invective against societies with private property as being 'conspiracies of the rich'.

In 2016, a major exhibition in London celebrated the five-hundredth anniversary of the publication of *Utopia*. A specially designed utopian flag – a smiley face on a bright yellow background – was raised above Somerset House, not far from the legal quarter where More began his career. A utopian fanfare was performed by the National Youth Orchestra. The artist Stephen Walter exhibited *Nova Utopia*, a new map of a fantastical island that contained utopian and dystopian motifs, and explored the encroachment of the private on the public sphere in contemporary society. The festival included workshops that invited participants to think about what the perfect society meant to them.

For conservatives, More's *Utopia* continues to be a symbol of anti-freedom and collectivism that has inspired centuries of wrong thinking. Defenders say that far from offering a rigid social blueprint, *Utopia* is an invitation to dream. Today we would be unlikely to accept a utopia that did not allow for diversity and dissent.

In its exploration of an alternative present through the voices of a rich cast of characters, More asks us to imagine new possibilities in a world of varied humans who may not always agree. In today's dizzyingly complex societies, riven by distrust and under increasing stress, this is the ambitious but clear-sighted principle for healing and renewal that More's *Utopia* offers us.

A Note on the Translation

With its author one of the most famous figures in English history, it may come as a surprise to new readers of *Utopia* that the work was written in Latin. The first English translation was not made until after More's death.

Research on Thomas More remains lively and there have been multiple translations of *Utopia*, continuing into the twenty-first century.

In this Capstone edition we use an early translation, that of Gilbert Burnet of 1684. The Burnet text is the original, but we have revised the paragraph layout slightly to increase readability.

Burnet was instrumental in overhauling More's reputation for Anglican Britain, claiming that because More wanted church reform and was highly critical of England's clerics – themes that appear in *Utopia* – he was in fact a forerunner of England's Protestants. Burnet emphasized the religious aspects of *Utopia* at the expense of those social ones that more recent scholars have placed at the centre of their interpretations. He hailed More as a man full of 'justice, contempt for money, humility, and a true generosity of mind'.

REFERENCES

Baker-Smith, Dominic, *More's Utopia* (London, 1991).

Chambers, R.W., *Thomas More* (London, 1935).

Elton, G.R., *Studies in Tudor and Stuart Politics and Government* (Cambridge, 1974–92).

Kautsky, Karl, translated by H.J. Stenning, *Thomas More and his Utopia* (New York, 1927).

McCutcheon, Elizabeth, *Liber Amicorum: A Collection of Essays by Elizabeth McCutcheon*, special issue of *Moreana*, Vol. 52, No. 201–202, *Issue* 3–4, December 2015.

Marius, Richard, *Thomas More* (New York, 1984).

Ridley, Jasper, *The Statesman and the Fanatic: Thomas Wolsey and Thomas More* (London, 1982).

ABOUT NIALL KISHTAINY

Niall Kishtainy is a writer with interests in economics and in the history of ideas. He holds a PhD in economics from the University of Warwick and has taught economic history at the London School of Economics. His most recent book, *A Little History of Economics*, was published by Yale University Press in 2017. He is currently working on a book on the history of London's utopians.

UTOPIA

CONTENTS

I

LETTER: THOMAS MORE TO PETER GILES

I am almost ashamed, right well-beloved Peter Giles, to send you this book of the Utopian commonwealth, well nigh after a year's space, which I am sure you looked for within a month and a half. And no marvel. For you know well enough that I was already disburdened of all the labour and study belonging to the invention of this work, and that I had no need at all to trouble my brains about the disposition or conveyance of that matter and, therefore, had nothing else to do but only to rehearse those things which you and I together heard Master Raphael tell and declare. Wherefore there was no cause why I should study to set forth the matter with eloquence; for as much as his talk could not be fine and eloquent, being first not studied for but sudden and unpremeditated, and then, as you know, of a man better seen in the Greek language then in the Latin tongue. And my writing, the nearer it should approach his homely, plain, and simple speech, so much the nearer should it go to the truth; which is the only mark, where unto I do and ought to direct all my travail and study herein.

I grant and confess, friend Peter, myself discharged of so much labour, having all these things ready done to my hand, that almost there was nothing left for me to do. Else either the invention, or the disposition of this matter, might have required of a wit neither base nor at all unlearned, both some time and leisure, and also some study. But if it was requisite and necessary that the matter should also have been written eloquently, and not alone truly, of a surety that thing I could have performed by no time or study. But now, seeing all these cares, stays, and hindrances were taken away, wherein else so much labour and study should have been employed, and that there remained no other thing for me to do but only to write plainly the matter as I heard it spoken, that indeed was a thing light and easy to be done. Howbeit, to the dispatching of this so little business my other cares and troubles did leave almost less than no leisure. While I do daily bestow my time about law matters; some to plead, some to hear, some as an arbitrator with mine award to determine, some as an umpire or a judge with my sentence finally to discuss; while I go one way to see and visit my friend, another way about mine own private affairs; while I spend almost all the day abroad amongst others and then reside at home among mine own, I leave to my myself, I mean to my book, no time.

For when I come home, I must commune with my wife, chat with my children, and talk with my servants. All the which things I reckon and account among business, forasmuch as they must of necessity be done; and done must they need be unless a man will be a stranger in his own house. And, in any wise, a man must so fashion and order his conditions, and so appoint and dispose himself, that he be merry, jocund, and pleasant among them whom either nature has provided, or chance has made, or he himself has chosen to be the fellows and companions of his life: so that with too much gentle behaviour and familiarity he do not mar them, and by too much sufferance of his servants make them his masters. Among these things now rehearsed steal away the day, the month, the year. When do I write then? And all this while I have spoken no word of sleep, neither yet of meals, which among a great number do waste no less time than does sleep, wherein almost half the time of man creepeth away. I, therefore, do win and get only that time which I steal from sleep and meals. Which time, because it is very little, and yet somewhat it is, therefore have I once at the last, though it be long first, finished *Utopia* and have sent it to you Peter to read and peruse to the intent that if anything has escaped me you might put me in remembrance of it. For though in this behalf I do not greatly mistrust myself (which would God I were somewhat in wit and learning, as I am not all of the worst and dullest in memory), yet have I not so great trust and confidence in it that I think nothing could fall out of my mind.

For John Clement, my boy, who as you know was there present with us, whom I suffer to be away from no talk wherein may be any profit or goodness (for out of this young-bladed and new-shot-up corn, which has already begun to spring up both in Latin and

Greek language, I look for plentiful increase at length of goodly ripe grain), he, I say, has brought me into great doubt. For whereas Hythloday (unless my memory fail me) said that the bridge of Amaurot, which goes over the river of Anyder, is five hundred paces, that is to say, half a mile, in length; my John saith that two hundred of these paces must be plucked away, for that the river contains there not above three hundred paces in breadth. I pray you heartily call the matter to your remembrance. For if you agree with him I also will say as you say and confess myself deceived. But if you cannot remember the thing, then surely I will write as I have done, and as mine own remembrance serves me. For as I shall take good heed that there be in my book nothing false, so if there be anything in doubt I will rather tell a lie then make a lie, because I had rather be good than wise.

Howbeit, this matter may easily be remedied if you will take the pains to ask the question of Raphael himself, by word of mouth if he be now with you, or else by your letters; which you must need do for another doubt also, which has chanced through, whose fault I cannot tell, whether through mine or yours or Raphael's. For neither we remembered to inquire of him, nor he to tell us, in what part of that new world Utopia is situated; which thing I had rather have spent no small sum of money than it should thus have escaped us. As well for that I am ashamed to be ignorant of what sea that Island standeth whereof I write so long a treatise; as also because there be with us certain men, and especially one devout and godly man, who is exceeding desirous to go unto Utopia, not for a vain and curious desire to see news, but to the intent that he may further and increase our religion which is there already begun. And that he may the better accomplish and perform this his good intent, he is minded to procure that he may be sent there by the high Bishop, yes, and that he himself may be made Bishop of Utopia; being nothing scrupulous herein, that he may obtain this bishopric with suit. For he counteth that a godly suit which proceeds not of the desire of honour or lucre but only of a godly zeal.

Wherefore, I most earnestly desire you, friend Peter, to talk with Hythloday, if you can face to face, or else write letters to him, and so to work in this matter that in this, my book, there may be neither anything be found that is untrue, neither anything be lacking which is true. And I think verily it shall be well done that you show unto him the book itself, for if I have missed or failed in any point, or find any fault that has escaped me, no man can so well correct and amend it as he can, and yet that can he not do unless he peruse and read over my book written. Moreover, by this means shall you perceive whether he will be willing and content that I should undertake to put this work in writing. For if he be minded to publish and put forth his own labours and travails himself, perchance he would be loathe, and so would I also, that in publishing the Utopian commonwealth I should prevent and take from him the flower and grace of the novelty of this his history.

Howbeit, to say the very truth, I am not fully determined with myself whether I will put forth my book or no. For the natures of men be so divers, the fantasies of some so wayward, their minds so unkind, their judgments so corrupt that they which lead a merry and jocund life following their own sensual pleasures and carnal lusts, may seem to be in a much better state or case than they that vex and unquiet themselves with cares and studies for putting forth and publishing of something, that may be either profit or pleasure to others, which others nevertheless will disdainfully, scornfully, and unkindly accept the same. The most part of all be unlearned, and a great number hold learning in contempt. The rude and barbarous allow nothing but that which is very barbarous indeed. If it be one that has a little smack of learning, he rejects as homely and common-ware whatsoever is not stuffed full of old moth-eaten words and that be worn out of use. Some there be that have pleasure only in old rustic antiquities, and some only in their own doings. One is so sour, so crabbed, and so unpleasant that he can abide with no mirth or sport; another is so narrow between the shoulders, that he can bear no jests or taunts. Some silly poor souls be so afraid that at every snappish word their nose shall be bitten off that they stand in no less dread of every quick and sharp word than he that is bitten of a mad dog fears water. Some be so mutable and wavering that every hour they be in a new mind, saying one thing sitting and another thing standing. Another sort sits upon their ale benches, and there among their cups they give judgment of the wits of writers and with great authority they condemn even as please them every writer according to his writing in most spiteful manner mocking, louting, and flouting them: being themselves in the mean season safe and, as sayeth the proverb, out of all danger of gunshot. For why they be so smug and smooth that they have not so much as one hair of an honest man whereby one may take hold of them. There be, moreover, some so unkind and ungentle that though they take great pleasure and delectation in the work, yet for all that they can not find in their hearts to love the author thereof, nor to afford him a good word, being much like uncourteous, unthankful, and churlish guests, which when they have with good and dainty meats well filled their bellies, depart home giving no thanks to the feast-maker. Go your ways now, and make a costly feast at your own charges for guests so dainty-mouthed, so divers in taste, and besides that, of so unkind and unthankful natures.

But nevertheless, friend Peter, do I pray you with Hythloday as I willed you before, and as for this matter, I shall be at my liberty afterwards to take new advisement. Howbeit, seeing I have taken great pains and labour in writing the matter, if it may stand with his mind and pleasure, I will, as touching the edition or publishing of the book, follow the counsel and advice of my friends, and especially yours. Thus fare you well, right

heartily beloved friend Peter, with
your gentle wife; and love
me as you have ever done;
for I love you better
then I ever did.

II

LETTER: PETER GILES TO JEROME DE BUSLEYDEN

Thomas More, the singular ornament of this our age, as you yourself (right honorable Busleyden) can witness, to whom he is perfectly well known, sent unto me this other day the *Island of Utopia*, to very few as yet known, but most worthy which, as far excelling Plato's commonwealth, all people should be willing to know: especially of a man most eloquent, so finely set forth, so cunningly painted out, and so evidently subject to the eye, that as oft as I read it, me thinketh that I see somewhat more then when I heard Raphael Hythloday himself (for I was present at that talk as well as master More) uttering and pronouncing his own words. Yea, though the same man, according to his pure eloquence, did so open and declare the matter, that he might plainly enough appear to report not things which he had learned of others only by hearsay, but which he had with his own eyes presently seen, and thoroughly viewed, and wherein he had in no small time been conversant and abiding. A man truly, in my opinion, as touching the knowledge of regions, peoples, and worldly experience, much passing, yea, even the very famous and renowned traveller Ulysses, and indeed such a one: as for the space of these eight-hundred years past I think nature into the world brought not forth his like, in comparison of whom Vespucci may be thought to have seen nothing.

Moreover, whereas we be wont more effectually and pithily to declare and express things that we have seen than which we have but only heard, there was besides that in this man a certain peculiar grace and singular dexterity to describe and set forth a matter with-all. Yet the self same things as oft as I behold and consider them drawn and painted out with master More's pencil, I am therewith so moved, so delighted, so inflamed, and so rapt, that sometime methink I am presently conversant, even in the island of Utopia. And I promise you, I can scant believe that Raphael himself, by all that five years space that he was in Utopia abiding, saw there so much as here in master More's description is to be seen and perceived. Which description, with so many wonders and miraculous things is replenished, that I stand in great doubt whereat first and chiefly to muse or marvel: whether at the excellency of his perfect and sure memory, which could well nigh word by word rehearse so many things once only heard; or else at his singular prudence, who so well and wittily marked and bare away all the original causes and fountains (to the vulgar people commonly most unknown) whereof both issue and spring the mortal confusion and utter decay of a commonwealth, and also the advancement and wealthy state of the same may rise and grow; or else at the efficacy and pith of his word, which in so fine a Latin style, with such force of eloquence, hath couched together and comprised so many and divers matters, especially being a man continually encumbered with so many busy and troublesome cares, both public and private, as he is. Howbeit all these things cause you little to marvel (right honorable Busleyden) for that you are familiarly and throughly acquainted with the notable, yea, almost divine, wit of the man.

But now to proceed to other matters, I surely know nothing needful or requisite to be adjoined unto his writings. Only a meter of four verses written in the Utopian tongue which, after master More's departure, Hythloday by chance showed me that have I caused to be added thereto, with the Alphabet of the same nation, and have also garnished the margin of the book with certain notes.[3] For, as touching the situation of the island, that is to say in what part of the world Utopia stands, the ignorance and lack whereof not a little troubleth and grieveth master More, indeed Raphael left not that unspoken of. Howbeit, with very few words he lightly touched it, incidentally by the way passing it over, as meaning of likelihood to keep and reserve that to another place. And the same, I know not how, by a certain evil and unlucky chance escaped us both. For when Raphael was speaking thereof, one of master More's servants came to him and whispered in his ear. Wherefore, I being then of purpose more earnestly given to hear, one of the company, by reason of cold taken, I think, a-shipboard, coughed out so loud, that he took from my hearing certain of his words. But I will never stint, nor rest, until I have got the full and exact knowledge hereof; insomuch that I will be able perfectly to instruct you, not only in the longitude or true meridian of the island, but also in the just latitude thereof, that is to say in the sublevation or height of the pole in that region, if our friend Hythloday be in safety and alive. For we hear very uncertain news of him. Some report that he died in his journey homeward. Some again affirm that he returned to his country; but partly, for that he could not abide with the fashions of his country folk, and partly for that his mind and affection was altogether set and fixed upon Utopia, they say that he has taken his voyage thitherward again.

Now as touching this: that the name of this island is nowhere found among the old and ancient cosmographers, this doubt Hythloday himself very well dissolved. For why it is possible enough (quotes he) that the name which it had in old time was afterward changed, or else that they never had knowledge of this island; forasmuch as now in our time divers lands be found, which to the old geographers were unknown. Howbeit, what needeth it in this behalf to fortify the matter with arguments, seeing master More is author hereof sufficient? But whereas he doubteth of the edition or imprinting of the book, indeed herein I both commend, and also acknowledge the man's modesty. Howbeit unto me, it seems a work most unworthy to be long suppressed and most worthy to go abroad into the hands of men, yea, and under the title of your name to be published to the world: either because the singular endowments and qualities of master More be to no man better known than to you, or else because no man is more fit and meet than you, with good counsels to further and announce the commonwealth, wherein you have many years already continued and travailed with great glory and commendation, both of wisdom and knowledge, and also of integrity and uprightness. Thus, O liberal supporter of good learning, and flower of this our time, I bid you most heartily well to fare.

At Antwerp, 1516, the first day of November.

III

LETTER: THOMAS MORE TO PETER GILES

I was extremely pleased with the criticism of my work, with which you are acquainted, by a clever person, who put this dilemma about Utopia: "If the facts as reported are true, I see some absurdities in them; but if fictitious, I find More's finished judgment in some respects wanting." Whoever he was, I am much obliged to him, Peter; I suspect him to be learned, and I can see he is friendly. By this frank criticism he has obliged me more than anyone else since the appearance of the book. For in the first place, attracted by interest in me or the work, he seems not to have wearied of the labour, but read it all through, not perfunctorily and hastily, as priests go through the Hours, but so slowly and carefully as to pay attention to details.

Secondly, by objecting to some things, he has given a tacit approval to the rest. Finally, in the very words in which he censures me, he gives me more praise than all who have praised me of set purpose. For he shows that he thinks highly of me, when he complains of disappointment when he reads something not finished, since it would be more than I could hope if I did not write some things that are absurd among so many.

Yet if I may in my turn deal faithfully with him, I do not see why so sharp-eyed a critic, because he has detected some absurdities in the institutions of Utopia, or I have devised some things inexpedient in the framing of a constitution, should be so minded as if there were nothing absurd in the world, or as if any philosopher had ever ordered the state, or even his own house, without instituting something that had better be changed. Why, if the memory of great men were not hallowed by time, I could in each of them quote points, in the condemnation of which I should get a unanimous vote. Now, when he doubts whether Utopia is real or fictitious, I find his finished judgment wanting.

I do not pretend that if I had determined to write about the commonwealth and had remembered such a story, I should have shrunk from a fiction, by which the truth, as if smeared with honey, might more pleasantly flow into men's minds. But if I wanted to abuse the ignorance of common folk, I should certainly have been careful to prefix some indications for the learned to see through my purpose. Thus if I had put nothing but the names of prince, river, city and island such as might suggest to the learned that the island was nowhere, the city a phantom, the river without water, and the prince without a people, this would not have been hard to do, and would have been much wittier than what I did; for if the faithfulness of an historian had not been binding on me, I am not so stupid as to have preferred to use those barbarous and meaningless names, Utopia, Anyder, Amaurot and Ademus.

But, Giles, since I see some people are so wary, that they can hardly be induced to believe what we simple and credulous folk have written down on the relation of Hythloday, lest my credit be in danger with them as well as the faithfulness of history, I am glad I may say on behalf of my offspring, what in Terence Mysis says about Glycerium's boy, lest he should be regarded as a changeling: "I thank the gods that some free women were present when I was brought to bed." For this also has fallen out very conveniently, that Raphael told his tale not merely to you but to many other respectable and worthy men, perhaps still more lengthily and weightily, certainly no less so, than he did to ourselves.

But if these unbelievers will not believe them either, let them go to Hythloday himself; for he is not yet dead. I heard lately from some who came from Portugal, that on March 1st last he was as hale and sprightly as ever. So let them inquire the truth of him or, if they like, try him with questions, only I would have them understand that I am only responsible for my part and not for the credit of another.

Farewell, dear Peter, and greet for me your charming wife and pretty little daughter, to whom my wife wishes long life.

IV

"UTOPIA"

A short meter by Anemolius, poet laureate and nephew to Hythloday:

Me, Utopia, called in Antiquity, void of haunt and harbour.

Now I am like to Plato's city, Whose fame flies the world through.

Yea like, or rather more likely, Plato's plot to excel and pass.

For what Plato's pen has plotted briefly, In naked words, as in a glass, The same have I performed fully, With laws, with men, and treasure fitly.

Wherefore not Utopia, but rather rightly, My name is Eutopie: a place of felicity.

Utopian alphabet, 1516 First Edition

VTOPIENSIVM ALPHABETVM.

a b c d e f g h i k l m n o p q r s t v x y

ò⊖ⱷ⊝⊖⊙⊃ⲥ Ⲟ⊍Ϛ ⵊ ⊿ Ⳑ Ⳇ ⳆⳆ Ⳝ ⵌ ⵎ Ⳡ Ⳝ Ⳝ

Tetrastichon vernacula Vtopiensium lingua.

Vtopos	ha	Boccas	peu	la

chama   polta   chamaan

Bargol   he   maglomi   baccan

soma   gymno   sophaon

Agrama   gymnosophon   labarembacha

bodamilomin

Voluala   barchin   heman   la

Iauoluola   dramme   pagloni.

Horum versuum ad verbum hæc est sententia.

Vtopus me dux ex non insula fecit insulam

Vna ego terrarum omnium absq; philosophia

Ciuitatem philosophicam expressi mortalibus

Libéter impartio mea, nó grauatim accipio meliora.

28

A Meter of Four Verses in the Utopian Tongue

Briefly Touching As Well the Strange Beginning, As Also The Happy and Wealth Continuance, of the Same Commonwealth[1]

Utopos ha Boccas peu la chama polta chamaan.

Bargol he maglomi baccan ſoma gymno ſophaon.

Agrama gymnoſophon labarembacha bodamilomin.

Voluala barchin heman la lauoluola dramme pagloni.

Which verses the translator, according to his simple knowledge and mean understanding in the Utopian tongue, hath thus rudely Englished:

My king and conqueror Utopus by name,

A prince of much renown and immortal fame,

Has made me an isle that once no island was,

Full fraught with worldly wealth, with pleasure and solace.

---

[1]This meter appeared in the first, 1516 edition of *Utopia*. Probably written by More's friend Peter Giles, its aim – along with the Utopian map and alphabet – was to give readers the sense that this imaginary land was real.

Utopia

I one of all other without philosophy,
Have shaped for many a philosophical city.
And mine I have nothing dangerous to impart,
So better to receive I am ready with all my heart.

V

BOOK ONE

Henry VIII, the unconquered King of England, a prince adorned with all the virtues that become a great monarch, having some differences of no small consequence with Charles the most serene Prince of Castile, sent me into Flanders, as his ambassador, for treating and composing matters between them.

I was colleague and companion to that incomparable man Cuthbert Tonstal, whom the King, with such universal applause, lately made Master of the Rolls; but of whom I will say nothing; not because I fear that the testimony of a friend will be suspected, but rather because his learning and virtues are too great for me to do them justice, and so well known, that they need not my commendations, unless I would, according to the proverb, "Show the sun with a lantern."

Those that were appointed by the Prince to treat with us, met us at Bruges, according to agreement; they were all worthy men. The Margrave of Bruges was their head, and the chief man among them; but he that was esteemed the wisest, and that spoke for the rest, was George Temse, the Provost of Casselsee: both art and nature had concurred to make him eloquent: he was very learned in the law; and, as he had a great capacity, so, by a long practice in affairs, he was very dexterous at unravelling them. After we had several times met, without coming to an agreement, they went to Brussels for some days, to know the Prince's pleasure; and, since our business would admit it, I went to Antwerp.

While I was there, among many that visited me, there was one that was more acceptable to me than any other, Peter Giles, born at Antwerp, who is a man of great honour, and of a good rank in his town, though less than he deserves; for I do not know if there be anywhere to be found a more learned and a better bred young man; for as he is both a very worthy and a very knowing person, so he is so civil to all men, so particularly kind to his friends, and so full of candour and affection, that there is not, perhaps, above one or two anywhere to be found, that is in all respects so perfect a friend: he is extraordinarily modest, there is no artifice in him, and yet no man has more of a prudent simplicity. His conversation was so pleasant and so innocently cheerful, that his company in a great measure lessened any longings to go back to my country, and to my wife and children, which an absence of four months had quickened very much.

One day, as I was returning home from mass at St. Mary's, which is the chief church, and the most frequented of any in Antwerp, I saw him, by accident, talking with a stranger, who seemed past the flower of his age; his face was tanned, he had a long beard, and his cloak was hanging carelessly about him, so that, by his looks and habit, I concluded he was a seaman. As soon as Peter saw me, he came and saluted me, and as I was returning his civility, he took me aside, and pointing to him with whom he had been discoursing, he said, "Do you see that man? I was just thinking to bring him to you."

I answered, "He should have been very welcome on your account."

"And on his own too," replied he, "if you knew the man, for there is none alive that can give so copious an account of unknown nations and countries as he can do, which I know you very much desire."

"Then," said I, "I did not guess amiss, for at first sight I took him for a seaman."

"But you are much mistaken," said he, "for he has not sailed as a seaman, but as a traveller, or rather a philosopher. This Raphael, who from his family carries the name of Hythloday, is not ignorant of the Latin tongue, but is eminently learned in the Greek, having applied himself more particularly to that than to the former, because he had given himself much to philosophy, in which he knew that the Romans have left us nothing that is valuable, except what is to be found in Seneca and Cicero. He is a Portuguese by birth, and was so desirous of seeing the world, that he divided his estate among his brothers, ran the same hazard as Americus Vesputius, and bore a share in three of his four voyages that are now published; only he did not return with him in his last, but obtained leave of him, almost by force, that he might be one of those twenty-four who were left at the farthest place at which they touched in their last voyage to New Castile. The leaving him thus did not a little gratify one that was more fond of travelling than of returning home to be buried in his own country; for he used often to say, that the way to heaven was the same from all places, and he that had no grave had the heavens still over him. Yet this disposition of mind had cost him dear, if God had not been very gracious to him; for after he, with five Castalians, had travelled over many countries, at last, by strange good fortune, he got to Ceylon, and from thence to Calicut, where he, very happily, found some Portuguese ships; and, beyond all men's expectations, returned to his native country."

When Peter had said this to me, I thanked him for his kindness in intending to give me the acquaintance of a man whose conversation he knew would be so acceptable; and upon that Raphael and I embraced each other. After those civilities were past which are usual with strangers upon their first meeting, we all went to my house, and entering into the garden, sat down on a green bank and entertained one another in discourse.

He told us that when Vesputius had sailed away, he, and his companions that stayed behind in New

Castile, by degrees insinuated themselves into the affections of the people of the country, meeting often with them and treating them gently; and at last they not only lived among them without danger, but conversed familiarly with them, and got so far into the heart of a prince, whose name and country I have forgot, that he both furnished them plentifully with all things necessary, and also with the conveniences of travelling, both boats when they went by water, and waggons when they travelled over land: he sent with them a very faithful guide, who was to introduce and recommend them to such other princes as they had a mind to see: and after many days' journey, they came to towns, and cities, and to commonwealths, that were both happily governed and well peopled.

Under the equator, and as far on both sides of it as the sun moves, there lay vast deserts that were parched with the perpetual heat of the sun; the soil was withered, all things looked dismally, and all places were either quite uninhabited, or abounded with wild beasts and serpents, and some few men, that were neither less wild nor less cruel than the beasts themselves. But, as they went farther, a new scene opened, all things grew milder, the air less burning, the soil more verdant, and even the beasts were less wild: and, at last, there were nations, towns, and cities, that had not only mutual commerce among themselves and with their neighbours, but traded, both by sea and land, to very remote countries. There they found the conveniences of seeing many countries on all hands, for no ship went any voyage into which he and his companions were not very welcome.

The first vessels that they saw were flat-bottomed, their sails were made of reeds and wicker, woven close together, only some were of leather; but, afterwards, they found ships made with round keels and canvas sails, and in all respects like our ships, and the seamen understood both astronomy and navigation. He got wonderfully into their favour by showing them the use of the needle, of which till then they were utterly ignorant. They sailed before with great caution, and only in summer time; but now they count all seasons alike, trusting wholly to the loadstone, in which they are, perhaps, more secure than safe; so that there is reason to fear that this discovery, which was thought would prove so much to their advantage, may, by their imprudence, become an occasion of much mischief to them.

But it were too long to dwell on all that he told us he had observed in every place, it would be too great a digression from our present purpose: whatever is necessary to be told concerning those wise and prudent institutions which he observed among civilised nations, may perhaps be related by us on a more proper occasion. We asked him many questions concerning all these things, to which he answered very willingly; we made no inquiries after monsters, than which nothing is more common; for everywhere one may hear of ravenous dogs and wolves, and cruel men-eaters, but it is not so easy to find states that are well and wisely governed.

As he told us of many things that were amiss in those new-discovered countries, so he reckoned up not a few things, from which patterns might be taken for correcting the errors of these nations among whom we live; of which an account may be given, as I have already promised, at some other time; for, at present, I intend only to relate those particulars that he told us, of the manners and laws of the Utopians: but I will begin with the occasion that led us to speak of that commonwealth.

After Raphael had discoursed with great judgment on the many errors that were both among us and these nations, had treated of the wise institutions both here and there, and had spoken as distinctly of the customs and government of every nation through which he had past, as if he had spent his whole life in it, Peter, being struck with admiration, said, "I wonder, Raphael, how it comes that you enter into no king's service, for I am sure there are none to whom you would not be very acceptable; for your learning and knowledge, both of men and things, is such, that you would not only entertain them very pleasantly, but be of great use to them, by the examples you could set before them, and the advices you could give them; and by this means you would both serve your own interest, and be of great use to all your friends."

"As for my friends," answered he, "I need not be much concerned, having already done for them all that was incumbent on me; for when I was not only in good health, but fresh and young, I distributed that among my kindred and friends which other people do not part with till they are old and sick: when they then unwillingly give that which they can enjoy no longer themselves. I think my friends ought to rest contented with this, and not to expect that for their sakes I should enslave myself to any king whatsoever."

"Soft and fair!" said Peter; "I do not mean that you should be a slave to any king, but only that you should assist them and be useful to them."

"The change of the word," said he, "does not alter the matter."

"But term it as you will," replied Peter, "I do not see any other way in which you can be so useful, both in private to your friends and to the public, and by which you can make your own condition happier."

"Happier?" answered Raphael, "is that to be compassed in a way so abhorrent to my genius? Now I live as I will, to which I believe, few courtiers can pretend; and there are so many that court the favour of great men, that there will be no great loss if they are not troubled either with me or with others of my temper."

Upon this, said I, "I perceive, Raphael, that you neither desire wealth nor greatness; and, indeed, I value and admire such a man much more than I do any of the great men in the world. Yet I think you would do what would well become so generous and philosophical a soul as yours is, if you would apply your time and thoughts to public affairs, even though you may happen to find it a little uneasy to yourself; and this you can never do with so much advantage as by being taken into the council of some great prince and putting him on noble and worthy actions, which I know you would do if you were in such a post; for the springs both of good and evil flow from the prince over a whole nation, as from a lasting fountain. So much learning as you have, even without practice in affairs, or so great a practice as you have had, without any other learning, would render you a very fit counsellor to any king whatsoever."

"You are doubly mistaken," said he, "Mr. More, both in your opinion of me and in the judgment you make of things: for as I have not that capacity that you fancy I have, so if I had it, the public would not be one jot the better when I had sacrificed my quiet to it. For most princes apply themselves more to affairs of war than to the useful arts of peace; and in these I neither have any knowledge, nor do I much desire it; they are generally more set on acquiring new kingdoms, right or wrong, than on governing well those they possess: and, among the ministers of princes, there are none that are not so wise as to need no assistance, or at least, that do not think themselves so wise that they imagine they need none; and if they court any, it is only those for whom the prince has much personal favour, whom by their fawning and flatteries they endeavour to fix to their own interests; and, indeed, nature has so made us, that we all love to be flattered and to please ourselves with our own notions: the old crow loves his young, and the ape her cubs. Now if in such a court, made up of persons who envy all others and only admire themselves, a person should but propose anything that he had either read in history or observed in his travels, the rest would think that the reputation of their wisdom would sink, and that their interests would be much depressed if they could not run it down: and, if all other things failed, then they would fly to this, that such or such things pleased our ancestors, and it were well for us if we could but match them. They would set up their rest on such an answer, as a sufficient confutation of all that could be said, as if it were a great misfortune that any should be found wiser than his ancestors. But though they willingly let go all the good things that were among those of former ages, yet, if better things are proposed, they cover themselves obstinately with this excuse of reverence to past times. I have met with these proud, morose, and absurd judgments of things in many places, particularly once in England."

"Were you ever there?" said I.

"Yes, I was," answered he, "and stayed some months there, not long after the rebellion in the West was suppressed, with a great slaughter of the poor people that were engaged in it.

"I was then much obliged to that reverend prelate, John Morton, Archbishop of Canterbury, Cardinal, and Chancellor of England; a man," said he, "Peter (for Mr. More knows well what he was), that was not less venerable for his wisdom and virtues than for the high character he bore: he was of a middle stature, not broken with age; his looks begot reverence rather than fear; his conversation was easy, but serious and grave; he sometimes took pleasure to try the force of those that came as suitors to him upon business by speaking sharply, though decently, to them, and by that he discovered their spirit and presence of mind; with which he was much delighted when it did not grow up to impudence, as bearing a great resemblance to his own temper, and he looked on such persons as the fittest men for affairs. He spoke both gracefully and weightily; he was eminently skilled in the law, had a vast understanding, and a prodigious memory; and those excellent talents with which nature had furnished him were improved by study and experience. When I was in England the King depended much on his counsels, and the Government seemed to be chiefly supported by him; for from his youth he had been all along practised in affairs; and, having passed through many traverses of fortune, he had, with great cost, acquired a vast stock of wisdom, which is not soon lost when it is purchased so dear.

"One day, when I was dining with him, there happened to be at table one of the English lawyers, who took occasion to run out in a high commendation of the severe execution of justice upon thieves, 'who,' as he said, 'were then hanged so fast that there were sometimes twenty on one gibbet!' and, upon that, he said, 'he could not wonder enough how it came to pass that, since so few escaped, there were yet so many thieves left, who were still robbing in all places.'

"Upon this, I (who took the boldness to speak freely before the Cardinal) said, 'There was no reason to wonder at the matter, since this way of punishing thieves was neither just in itself nor good for the public; for, as the severity was too great, so the remedy was not effectual; simple theft not being so great a crime that it ought to cost a man his life;

no punishment, how severe soever, being able to restrain those from robbing who can find out no other way of livelihood. In this,' said I, 'not only you in England, but a great part of the world, imitate some ill masters, that are readier to chastise their scholars than to teach them. There are dreadful punishments enacted against thieves, but it were much better to make such good provisions by which every man might be put in a method how to live, and so be preserved from the fatal necessity of stealing and of dying for it.'

"'There has been care enough taken for that,' said he; 'there are many handicrafts, and there is husbandry, by which they may make a shift to live, unless they have a greater mind to follow ill courses.'

"'That will not serve your turn,' said I, 'for many lose their limbs in civil or foreign wars, as lately in the Cornish rebellion, and some time ago in your wars with France, who, being thus mutilated in the service of their king and country, can no more follow their old trades, and are too old to learn new ones; but since wars are only accidental things, and have intervals, let us consider those things that fall out every day. There is a great number of noblemen among you that are themselves as idle as drones, that subsist on other men's labour, on the labour of their tenants, whom, to raise their revenues, they pare to the quick. This, indeed, is the only instance of their frugality, for in all other things they are prodigal, even to the beggaring of themselves; but, besides this, they carry about with them a great number of idle fellows, who never learned any art by which they may gain their living; and these, as soon as either their lord dies, or they themselves fall sick, are turned out of doors; for your lords are readier to feed idle people than to take care of the sick; and often the heir is not able to keep together so great a family as his predecessor did. Now, when the stomachs of those that are thus turned out of doors grow keen, they rob no less keenly; and what else can they do? For when, by wandering about, they have worn out both their health and their clothes, and are tattered, and look ghastly, men of quality will not entertain them, and poor men dare not do it, knowing that one who has been bred up in idleness and plea-sure, and who was used to walk about with his sword and buckler, despising all the neighbourhood with an insolent scorn as far below him, is not fit for the spade and mattock; nor will he serve a poor man for so small a hire and in so low a diet as he can afford to give him.'

"To this he answered, 'This sort of men ought to be particularly cherished, for in them consists the force of the armies for which we have occasion; since their birth inspires them with a nobler sense of honour than is to be found among tradesmen or ploughmen.'

"'You may as well say,' replied I, 'that you must cherish thieves on the account of wars, for you will never want the one as long as you have the other; and as robbers prove sometimes gallant soldiers, so soldiers often prove brave robbers, so near an alliance there is between those two sorts of life. But this bad custom, so common among you, of keeping many servants, is not peculiar to this nation. In France there is yet a more pestiferous sort of people, for the whole country is full of soldiers, still kept up in time of peace (if such a state of a nation can be called a peace); and these are kept in pay upon the same account that you plead for those idle retainers about noblemen: this being a maxim of those pretended statesmen, that it is necessary for the public safety to have a good body of veteran soldiers ever in readiness. They think raw men are not to be depended on, and they sometimes seek occasions for making war, that they may train up their soldiers in the art of cutting throats, or, as Sallust observed, "for keeping their hands in use, that they may not grow dull by too long an intermission." But France has learned to its cost how dangerous it is to feed such beasts. The fate of the Romans, Carthaginians, and Syrians, and many other nations and cities, which were both overturned and quite ruined by those standing armies, should make others wiser; and the folly of this maxim of the French appears plainly even from this, that their trained soldiers often find your raw men prove too hard for them, of which I will not

47

say much, lest you may think I flatter the English. Every day's experience shows that the mechanics in the towns or the clowns in the country are not afraid of fighting with those idle gentlemen, if they are not disabled by some misfortune in their body or dispirited by extreme want; so that you need not fear that those well-shaped and strong men (for it is only such that noblemen love to keep about them till they spoil them), who now grow feeble with ease and are softened with their effeminate manner of life, would be less fit for action if they were well bred and well employed. And it seems very unreasonable that, for the prospect of a war, which you need never have but when you please, you should maintain so many idle men, as will always disturb you in time of peace, which is ever to be more considered than war. But I do not think that this necessity of stealing arises only from hence; there is another cause of it, more peculiar to England.'

"'What is that?' said the Cardinal.

"'The increase of pasture,' said I, 'by which your sheep, which are naturally mild, and easily kept in order, may be said now to devour men and unpeople, not only villages, but towns; for wherever it is found that the sheep of any soil yield a softer and richer wool than ordinary, there the nobility and gentry, and even those holy men, the abbots! not contented with the old rents which their farms yielded, nor thinking it enough that they, living at their ease, do no good to the public, resolve to do it hurt instead of good. They stop the course of agriculture, destroying houses and towns, reserving only the churches, and enclose grounds that they may lodge their sheep in them. As if forests and parks had swallowed up too little of the land, those worthy countrymen turn the best inhabited places into solitudes; for when an insatiable wretch, who is a plague to his country, resolves to enclose many thousand acres of ground, the owners, as well as tenants, are turned out of their possessions by trick or by main force, or, being wearied out by ill usage, they are forced to sell them; by which means those miserable people, both men and women, married and unmarried, old and young, with their poor but numerous families (since country business requires many hands), are all forced to change their seats, not knowing whither to go; and they must sell, almost for nothing, their household stuff, which could not bring them much money, even though they might stay for a buyer. When that little money is at an end (for it will be soon spent), what is left for them to do but either to steal, and so to be hanged (God knows how justly!), or to go about and beg? and if they do this they are put in prison as idle vagabonds, while they would willingly work but can find none that will hire them; for there is no more occasion for country labour, to which they have been bred, when there is no arable ground left. One shepherd can look after a flock, which will stock an extent of ground that would require many hands if it were to be ploughed and reaped.

"'This, likewise, in many places raises the price of corn. The price of wool is also so risen that the poor people, who were wont to make cloth, are no more able to buy it; and this, likewise, makes many of them idle: for since the increase of pasture God has punished the avarice of the owners by a rot among the sheep, which has destroyed vast numbers of them–to us it might have seemed more just had it fell on the owners themselves. But, suppose the sheep should increase ever so much, their price is not likely to fall; since, though they cannot be called a monopoly, because they are not engrossed by one person, yet they are in so few hands, and these are so rich, that, as they are not pressed to sell them sooner than they have a mind to it, so they never do it till they have raised the price as high as possible.

"'And on the same account it is that the other kinds of cattle are so dear, because many villages being pulled down, and all country labour being much neglected, there are none who make it their business to breed them. The rich do not breed cattle as they do sheep, but buy them lean and at low prices; and, after they have fattened them on their grounds, sell them again at high rates. And I do not think that all the inconveniences this will produce are yet observed; for, as they sell the cattle dear, so, if they are consumed faster than the breeding countries from which they are brought can afford them, then the stock must decrease, and this must needs end in great scarcity; and by these means, this your island, which seemed as to this particular the happiest in the world, will suffer much by the cursed avarice of a few persons: besides this, the rising of corn makes all people lessen their families as much as they can; and what can those who are dismissed by them do but either beg or rob? And to this last a man of a great mind is much sooner drawn than to the former.

"'Luxury likewise breaks in apace upon you to set forward your poverty and misery; there is an excessive vanity in apparel, and great cost in diet, and that not only in noblemen's families, but even among tradesmen, among the farmers themselves, and among all ranks of persons. You have also many infamous houses, and, besides those that are known, the taverns and ale-houses are no better; add to these dice, cards, tables, football, tennis, and quoits, in which money runs fast away; and those that are initiated into them must, in the conclusion, betake themselves to robbing for a supply. Banish these plagues, and give orders that those who have dispeopled so much soil may either rebuild the villages they have pulled down or let out their grounds to such as will do it; restrain those engrossings of the rich, that are as bad almost as monopolies; leave fewer occasions to idleness; let agriculture be set up again, and the manufacture of the wool be regulated, that so there may be work found for those companies of idle people whom want forces to be thieves, or who now, being idle vagabonds or useless servants, will certainly grow thieves at last. If you do not find a remedy to these evils it is a vain thing to boast of your severity in punishing theft, which, though it may have the appearance of justice, yet in itself is neither just nor convenient; for if you suffer your people to be ill-educated, and their manners to be corrupted from their infancy, and then punish them for those crimes to which their first education disposed them, what else is to be concluded from this but that you first make thieves and then punish them?'

"While I was talking thus, the Counsellor, who was present, had prepared an answer, and had resolved to resume all I had said, according to the formality of a debate, in which things are generally repeated more faithfully than they are answered, as if the chief trial to be made were of men's memories.

"'You have talked prettily, for a stranger,' said he, 'having heard of many things among us which you have not been able to consider well; but I will make the whole matter plain to you, and will first repeat in order all that you have said; then I will show how much your ignorance of our affairs has misled you; and will, in the last place, answer all your arguments. And, that I may begin where I promised, there were four things – '

"'Hold your peace!' said the Cardinal; 'this will take up too much time; therefore we will, at present, ease you of the trouble of answering, and reserve it to our next meeting, which shall be to-morrow, if Raphael's affairs and yours can admit of it. But, Raphael,' said he to me, 'I would gladly know upon what reason it is that you think theft ought not to be punished by death: would you give way to it? or do you propose any other punishment that will be more useful to the public? for, since death does not restrain theft, if men thought their lives would be safe, what fear or force could restrain ill men? On the contrary, they would look on the mitigation of the punishment as an invitation to commit more crimes.'

"I answered, 'It seems to me a very unjust thing to take away a man's life for a little money, for nothing in the world can be of equal value with a man's life: and if it be said, "that it is not for the money that one suffers, but for his breaking the law," I must say, extreme justice is an extreme injury: for we ought not to approve of those terrible laws that make the smallest offences capital, nor of that opinion of the Stoics that makes all crimes equal; as if there were no difference to be made between the killing a man and the taking his purse, between which, if we examine things impartially, there is no likeness nor proportion. God has commanded us not to kill, and shall we kill so easily for a little money? But if one shall say, that by that law we are only forbid to kill any except when the laws of the land allow of it, upon the same grounds, laws may be made, in some cases, to allow of adultery and perjury: for God having taken from us the right of disposing either of our own or of other people's lives, if it is pretended that the mutual consent of men in making laws can authorise man-slaughter in cases in which God has given us no example, that it frees people from the obligation of the divine law, and so makes murder a lawful action, what is this, but to give a preference to human laws before the divine? and, if this is once admitted, by the same rule men may, in all other things, put what restrictions they please upon the laws of God. If, by the Mosaical law, though it was rough and severe, as being a yoke laid on an obstinate and servile nation, men were only fined, and not put to death for theft, we cannot imagine, that in this new law of mercy, in which God treats us with the tenderness of a father, He has given us a greater licence to cruelty than He did to the Jews.

"'Upon these reasons it is, that I think putting thieves to death is not lawful; and it is plain and obvious that it is absurd and of ill consequence to the commonwealth that a thief and a murderer should be equally punished; for if a robber sees that his danger is the same if he is convicted of theft as if he were guilty of murder, this will naturally incite him to kill the person whom otherwise he would only have robbed; since, if the punishment is the same, there is more security, and less danger of discovery, when he that can best make it is put out of the way; so that terrifying thieves too much provokes them to cruelty.

"But as to the question, 'What more convenient way of punishment can be found?' I think it much easier to find out that than to invent anything that is worse; why should we doubt but the way that was so long in use among the old Romans, who understood so well the arts of government, was very proper for their punishment? They condemned such as they found guilty of great crimes to work their whole lives in quarries, or to dig in mines with chains about them. But the method that I liked best was that which I observed in my travels in Persia, among the Polylerits, who are a considerable and well-governed people: they pay a yearly tribute to the King of Persia, but in all other respects they are a free nation, and governed by their own laws: they lie far from the sea, and are environed with hills; and, being contented with the productions of their own country, which is very fruitful, they have little commerce with any other nation; and as they, according to the genius of their country, have no inclination to enlarge their borders, so their mountains and the pension they pay to the Persian, secure them from all invasions. Thus they have no wars among them; they live rather conveniently than with splendour, and may be rather called a happy nation than either eminent or famous; for I do not think that they are known, so much as by name, to any but their next neighbours.

"Those that are found guilty of theft among them are bound to make restitution to the owner, and not, as it is in other places, to the prince, for they reckon that the prince has no more right to the stolen goods than the thief; but if that which was stolen is no more in being, then the goods of the thieves are estimated, and restitution being made out of them, the remainder is given to their wives and children; and they themselves are condemned to serve in the public works, but are neither imprisoned nor chained, unless there happens to be some extraordinary circumstance in their crimes. They go about loose and free, working for the public: if they are idle or backward to work they are whipped, but if they work hard they are well used and treated without any mark of reproach; only the lists of them are called always at night, and then they are shut up. They suffer no other uneasiness but this of constant labour; for, as they work for the public, so they are well entertained out of the public stock, which is done differently in different places: in some places whatever is bestowed on them is raised by a charitable contribution; and, though this way may seem uncertain, yet so merciful are the inclinations of that people, that they are plentifully supplied by it; but in other places public revenues are set aside for them, or there is a constant tax or poll-money raised for their maintenance. In some places they are set to no public work, but every private man that has occasion to hire workmen goes to the market-places and hires them of the public, a little lower than he would do a freeman. If they go lazily about their task he may quicken them with the whip. By this means there is always some piece of work or other to be done by them; and, besides their livelihood, they earn somewhat still to the public.

"'They all wear a peculiar habit, of one certain colour, and their hair is cropped a little above their ears, and a piece of one of their ears is cut off. Their friends are allowed to give them either meat, drink, or clothes, so they are of their proper colour; but it is death, both to the giver and taker, if they give them money; nor is it less penal for any freeman to take money from them upon any account whatsoever: and it is also death for any of these slaves (so they are called) to handle arms. Those of every division of the country are distinguished by a peculiar mark, which it is capital for them to lay aside, to go out of their bounds, or to talk with a slave of another jurisdiction, and the very attempt of an escape is no less penal than an escape itself. It is death for any other slave to be accessory to it; and if a freeman engages in it he is condemned to slavery. Those that discover it are rewarded–if freemen, in money; and if slaves, with liberty, together with a pardon for being accessory to it; that so they might find their account rather in repenting of their engaging in such a design than in persisting in it.

"'These are their laws and rules in relation to robbery, and it is obvious that they are as advantageous as they are mild and gentle; since vice is not only destroyed and men preserved, but they are treated in such a manner as to make them see the necessity of being honest and of employing the rest of their lives in repairing the injuries they had formerly done to society. Nor is there any hazard of their falling back to their old customs; and so little do travellers apprehend mischief from them that they generally make use of them for guides from one jurisdiction to another; for there is nothing left them by which they can rob or be the better for it, since, as they are disarmed, so the very having of money is a sufficient conviction: and as they are certainly punished if discovered, so they cannot hope to escape; for their habit being in all the parts of it different from what is commonly worn, they cannot fly away, unless they would go naked, and even then their cropped ear would betray them. The only danger to be feared from them is their conspiring against the government; but those of one division and neighbourhood can do nothing to any purpose unless a general conspiracy were laid amongst all the slaves of the several jurisdictions, which cannot be done, since they cannot meet or talk together; nor will any venture on a design where the concealment would be so dangerous and the discovery so profitable. None are quite hopeless of recovering their freedom, since by their obedience and patience, and by giving good grounds to believe that they will change their manner of life for the future, they may expect at last to obtain their liberty, and some are every year restored to it upon the good character that is given of them.

"When I had related all this, I added that I did not see why such a method might not be followed with more advantage than could ever be expected from that severe justice which the Counsellor magnified so much. To this he answered, 'That it could never take place in England without endangering the whole nation.'

"As he said this he shook his head, made some grimaces, and held his peace, while all the company seemed of his opinion, except the Cardinal, who said, 'That it was not easy to form a judgment of its success, since it was a method that never yet had been tried; but if,' said he, 'when sentence of death were passed upon a thief, the prince would reprieve him for a while, and make the experiment upon him, denying him the privilege of a sanctuary; and then, if it had a good effect upon him, it might take place; and, if it did not succeed, the worst would be to execute the sentence on the condemned persons at last; and I do not see,' added he, 'why it would be either unjust, inconvenient, or at all dangerous to admit of such a delay; in my opinion the vagabonds ought to be treated in the same manner, against whom, though we have made many laws, yet we have not been able to gain our end.'

"When the Cardinal had done, they all commended the motion, though they had despised it when it came from me, but more particularly commended what related to the vagabonds, because it was his own observation.

"I do not know whether it be worth while to tell what followed, for it was very ridiculous; but I shall venture at it, for as it is not foreign to this matter, so some good use may be made of it. There was a Jester standing by, that counterfeited the fool so naturally that he seemed to be really one; the jests which he offered were so cold and dull that we laughed more at him than at them, yet sometimes he said, as it were by chance, things that were not unpleasant, so as to justify the old proverb, 'That he who throws the dice often, will sometimes have a lucky hit.'

"When one of the company had said that I had taken care of the thieves, and the Cardinal had taken care of the vagabonds, so that there remained nothing but that some public provision might be made for the poor whom sickness or old age had disabled from labour, 'Leave that to me,' said the Fool, 'and I shall take care of them, for there is no sort of people whose sight I abhor more, having been so often vexed with them and with their sad complaints; but as dolefully soever as they have told their tale, they could never prevail so far as to draw one penny from me; for either I had no mind to give them anything, or, when I had a mind to do it, I had nothing to give them; and they now know me so well that they will not lose their labour, but let me pass without giving me any trouble, because they hope for nothing–no more, in faith, than if I were a priest; but I would have a law made for sending all these beggars to monasteries, the men to the Benedictines, to be made lay-brothers, and the women to be nuns.'

"The Cardinal smiled, and approved of it in jest, but the rest liked it in earnest. There was a divine present, who, though he was a grave morose man, yet he was so pleased with this reflection that was made on the priests and the monks that he began to play with the Fool, and said to him, 'This will not deliver you from all beggars, except you take care of us Friars.' 'That is done already,' answered the Fool, 'for the Cardinal has provided for you by what he proposed for restraining vagabonds and setting them to work, for I know no vagabonds like you.'

"This was well entertained by the whole company, who, looking at the Cardinal, perceived that he was not ill-pleased at it; only the Friar himself was vexed, as may be easily imagined, and fell into such a passion that he could not forbear railing at the Fool, and calling him knave, slanderer, backbiter, and son of perdition, and then cited some dreadful threatenings out of the Scriptures against him. Now the Jester thought he was in his element, and laid about him freely. 'Good Friar,' said he, 'be not angry, for it is written, "In patience possess your soul."'

"The Friar answered (for I shall give you his own words), 'I am not angry, you hangman; at least, I do not sin in it, for the Psalmist says, "Be ye angry and sin not."' Upon this the Cardinal admonished him gently, and wished him to govern his passions. 'No, my lord,' said he, 'I speak not but from a good zeal, which I ought to have, for holy men have had a good zeal, as it is said, "The zeal of thy house hath eaten me up;" and we sing in our church that those who mocked Elisha as he went up to the house of God felt the effects of his zeal, which that mocker, that rogue, that scoundrel, will perhaps feel.'

"'You do this, perhaps, with a good intention,' said the Cardinal, 'but, in my opinion, it were wiser in you, and perhaps better for you, not to engage in so ridiculous a contest with a Fool.'

"'No, my lord,' answered he, 'that were not wisely done, for Solomon, the wisest of men, said, "Answer a Fool according to his folly," which I now do, and show him the ditch into which he will fall, if he is not aware of it; for if the many mockers of Elisha, who was but one bald man, felt the effect of his zeal, what will become of the mocker of so many Friars, among whom there are so many bald men? We have, likewise, a bull, by which all that jeer us are excommunicated.'

"When the Cardinal saw that there was no end of this matter he made a sign to the Fool to withdraw, turned the discourse another way, and soon after rose from the table, and, dismissing us, went to hear causes.

"Thus, Mr. More, I have run out into a tedious story, of the length of which I had been ashamed, if (as you earnestly begged it of me) I had not observed you to hearken to it as if you had no mind to lose any part of it. I might have contracted it, but I resolved to give it you at large, that you might observe how those that despised what I had proposed, no sooner perceived that the Cardinal did not dislike it but presently approved of it, fawned so on him and flattered him to such a degree, that they in good earnest applauded those things that he only liked in jest; and from hence you may gather how little courtiers would value either me or my counsels."

To this I answered, "You have done me a great kindness in this relation; for as everything has been related by you both wisely and pleasantly, so you have made me imagine that I was in my own country and grown young again, by recalling that good Cardinal to my thoughts, in whose family I was bred from my childhood; and though you are, upon other accounts, very dear to me, yet you are the dearer because you honour his memory so much; but, after all this, I cannot change my opinion, for I still think that if you could overcome that aversion which you have to the courts of princes, you might, by the advice which it is in your power to give, do a great deal of good to mankind, and this is the chief design that every good man ought to propose to himself in living; for your friend Plato thinks that nations will be happy when either philosophers become kings or kings become philosophers. It is no wonder if we are so far from that happiness while philosophers will not think it their duty to assist kings with their counsels."

"They are not so base-minded," said he, "but that they would willingly do it; many of them have already done it by their books, if those that are in power would but hearken to their good advice. But Plato judged right, that except kings themselves became philosophers, they who from their childhood are corrupted with false notions would never fall in entirely with the counsels of philosophers, and this he himself found to be true in the person of Dionysius.

"Do not you think that if I were about any king, proposing good laws to him, and endeavouring to root out all the cursed seeds of evil that I found in him, I should either be turned out of his court, or, at least, be laughed at for my pains? For instance, what could I signify if I were about the King of France, and were called into his cabinet council, where several wise men, in his hearing, were proposing many expedients; as, by what arts and practices Milan may be kept, and Naples, that has so often slipped out of their hands, recovered; how the Venetians, and after them the rest of Italy, may be subdued; and then how Flanders, Brabant, and all Burgundy, and some other kingdoms which he has swallowed already in his designs, may be added to his empire? One proposes a league with the Venetians, to be kept as long as he finds his account in it, and that he ought to communicate counsels with them, and give them some share of the spoil till his success makes him need or fear them less, and then it will be easily taken out of their hands; another proposes the hiring the Germans and the securing the Switzers by pensions; another proposes the gaining the Emperor by money, which is omnipotent with him; another proposes a peace with the King of Arragon, and, in order to cement it, the yielding up the King of Navarre's pretensions; another thinks that the Prince of Castile is to be wrought on by the hope of an alliance, and that some of his courtiers are to be gained to the French faction by pensions. The hardest point of all is, what to do with England; a treaty of peace is to be set on foot, and, if their alliance is not to be depended on, yet it is to be made as firm as possible, and they are to be called friends, but suspected as enemies: therefore the Scots are to be kept in readiness to be let loose upon England on every occasion; and some banished nobleman is to be supported underhand (for by the League it cannot be done avowedly) who has a pretension to the crown, by which means that suspected prince may be kept in awe.

"Now when things are in so great a fermentation, and so many gallant men are joining counsels how to carry on the war, if so mean a man as I should stand up and wish them to change all their counsels–to let Italy alone and stay at home, since the kingdom of France was indeed greater than could be well governed by one man; that therefore he ought not to think of adding others to it; and if, after this, I should propose to them the resolutions of the Achorians, a people that lie on the south-east of Utopia, who long ago engaged in war in order to add to the dominions of their prince another kingdom, to which he had some pretensions by an ancient alliance: this they conquered, but found that the trouble of keeping it was equal to that by which it was gained; that the conquered people were always either in rebellion or exposed to foreign invasions, while they were obliged to be incessantly at war, either for or against them, and consequently could never disband their army; that in the meantime they were oppressed with taxes, their money went out of the kingdom, their blood was spilt for the glory of their king without procuring the least advantage to the people, who received not the smallest benefit from it even in time of peace; and that, their manners being corrupted by a long war, robbery and murders everywhere abounded, and their laws fell into contempt; while their king, distracted with the care of two kingdoms, was the less able to apply his mind to the interest of either. When they saw this, and that there would be no end to these evils, they by joint counsels made an humble address to their king, desiring him to choose which of the two kingdoms he had the greatest mind to keep, since he could not hold both; for they were too great a people to be governed by a divided king, since no man would willingly have a groom that should be in common between him and another. Upon which the good prince was forced to quit his new kingdom to one of his friends (who was not long after dethroned), and to be contented with his old one. To this I would add that after all those warlike attempts, the vast confusions, and the consumption both of treasure and of people that must follow them, perhaps upon some misfortune they might be forced to throw up all at last; therefore it seemed much more eligible that the king should improve his ancient kingdom all he could, and make it flourish as much as possible; that he should love his people, and be beloved of them; that he should live among them, govern them gently and let other kingdoms alone, since that which had fallen to his share was big enough, if not too big, for him:–pray, how do you think would such a speech as this be heard?"

"I confess," said I, "I think not very well."

"But what," said he, "if I should sort with another kind of ministers, whose chief contrivances and consultations were by what art the prince's treasures might be increased? where one proposes raising the value of specie when the king's debts are large, and lowering it when his revenues were to come in, that so he might both pay much with a little, and in a little receive a great deal. Another proposes a pretence of a war, that money might be raised in order to carry it on, and that a peace be concluded as soon as that was done; and this with such appearances of religion as might work on the people, and make them impute it to the piety of their prince, and to his tenderness for the lives of his subjects. A third offers some old musty laws that have been antiquated by a long disuse (and which, as they had been forgotten by all the subjects, so they had also been broken by them), and proposes the levying the penalties of these laws, that, as it would bring in a vast treasure, so there might be a very good pretence for it, since it would look like the executing a law and the doing of justice. A fourth proposes the prohibiting of many things under severe penalties, especially such as were against the interest of the people, and then the dispensing with these prohibitions, upon great compositions, to those who might find their advantage in breaking them. This would serve two ends, both of them acceptable to many; for as those whose avarice led them to transgress would be severely fined, so the selling licences dear would look as if a prince were tender of his people, and would not easily, or at low rates, dispense with anything that might be against the public good.

"Another proposes that the judges must be made sure, that they may declare always in favour of the prerogative; that they must be often sent for to court, that the king may hear them argue those points in which he is concerned; since, how unjust soever any of his pretensions may be, yet still some one or other of them, either out of contradiction to others, or the pride of singularity, or to make their court, would find out some pretence or other to give the king a fair colour to carry the point. For if the judges but differ in opinion, the clearest thing in the world is made by that means disputable, and truth being once brought in question, the king may then take advantage to expound the law for his own profit; while the judges that stand out will be brought over, either through fear or modesty; and they being thus gained, all of them may be sent to the Bench to give sentence boldly as the king would have it; for fair pretences will never be wanting when sentence is to be given in the prince's favour. It will either be said that equity lies of his side, or some words in the law will be found sounding that way, or some forced sense will be put on them; and, when all other things fail, the king's undoubted prerogative will be pretended, as that which is above all law, and to which a religious judge ought to have a special regard.

"Thus all consent to that maxim of Crassus, that a prince cannot have treasure enough, since he must maintain his armies out of it; that a king, even though he would, can do nothing unjustly; that all property is in him, not excepting the very persons of his subjects; and that no man has any other property but that which the king, out of his goodness, thinks fit to leave him. And they think it is the prince's interest that there be as little of this left as may be, as if it were his advantage that his people should have neither riches nor liberty, since these things make them less easy and willing to submit to a cruel and unjust government. Whereas necessity and poverty blunts them, makes them patient, beats them down, and breaks that height of spirit that might otherwise dispose them to rebel.

"Now what if, after all these propositions were made, I should rise up and assert that such counsels were both unbecoming a king and mischievous to him; and that not only his honour, but his safety, consisted more in his people's wealth than in his own; if I should show that they choose a king for their own sake, and not for his; that, by his care and endeavours, they may be both easy and safe; and that, therefore, a prince ought to take more care of his people's happiness than of his own, as a shepherd is to take more care of his flock than of himself?

"It is also certain that they are much mistaken that think the poverty of a nation is a mean of the public safety. Who quarrel more than beggars? who does more earnestly long for a change than he that is uneasy in his present circumstances? And who run to create confusions with so desperate a boldness as those who, having nothing to lose, hope to gain by them? If a king should fall under such contempt or envy that he could not keep his subjects in their duty but by oppression and ill usage, and by rendering them poor and miserable, it were certainly better for him to quit his kingdom than to retain it by such methods as make him, while he keeps the name of authority, lose the majesty due to it. Nor is it so becoming the dignity of a king to reign over beggars as over rich and happy subjects.

"And therefore Fabricius, a man of a noble and exalted temper, said 'He would rather govern rich men than be rich himself; since for one man to abound in wealth and pleasure when all about him are mourning and groaning, is to be a gaoler and not a king.' He is an unskilful physician that cannot cure one disease without casting his patient into another. So he that can find no other way for correcting the errors of his people but by taking from them the conveniences of life, shows that he knows not what it is to govern a free nation. He himself ought rather to shake off his sloth, or to lay down his pride, for the contempt or hatred that his people have for him takes its rise from the vices in himself. Let him live upon what belongs to him without wronging others, and accommodate his expense to his revenue. Let him punish crimes, and, by his wise conduct, let him endeavour to prevent them, rather than be severe when he has suffered them to be too common. Let him not rashly revive laws that are abrogated by disuse, especially if they have been long forgotten and never wanted. And let him never take any penalty for the breach of them to which a judge would not give way in a private man, but would look on him as a crafty and unjust person for pretending to it.

"To these things I would add that law among the Macarians–a people that live not far from Utopia–by which their king, on the day on which he began to reign, is tied by an oath, confirmed by solemn sacrifices, never to have at once above a thousand pounds of gold in his treasures, or so much silver as is equal to that in value. This law, they tell us, was made by an excellent king who had more regard to the riches of his country than to his own wealth, and therefore provided against the heaping up of so much treasure as might impoverish the people. He thought that moderate sum might be sufficient for any accident, if either the king had occasion for it against the rebels, or the kingdom against the invasion of an enemy; but that it was not enough to encourage a prince to invade other men's rights–a circumstance that was the chief cause of his making that law. He also thought that it was a good provision for that free circulation of money so necessary for the course of commerce and exchange. And when a king must distribute all those extraordinary accessions that increase treasure beyond the due pitch, it makes him less disposed to oppress his subjects. Such a king as this will be the terror of ill men, and will be beloved by all the good. If, I say, I should talk of these or such-like things to men that had taken their bias another way, how deaf would they be to all I could say!"

"No doubt, very deaf," answered I; "and no wonder, for one is never to offer propositions or advice that we are certain will not be entertained. Discourses so much out of the road could not avail anything, nor have any effect on men whose minds were prepossessed with different sentiments. This philosophical way of speculation is not unpleasant among friends in a free conversation; but there is no room for it in the courts of princes, where great affairs are carried on by authority."

"That is what I was saying," replied he, "that there is no room for philosophy in the courts of princes."

"Yes, there is," said I, "but not for this speculative philosophy, that makes everything to be alike fitting at all times; but there is another philosophy that is more pliable, that knows its proper scene, accommodates itself to it, and teaches a man with propriety and decency to act that part which has fallen to his share. If when one of Plautus' comedies is upon the stage, and a company of servants are acting their parts, you should come out in the garb of a philosopher, and repeat, out of *Octavia*, a discourse of Seneca's to Nero, would it not be better for you to say nothing than by mixing things of such different natures to make an impertinent tragicomedy? for you spoil and corrupt the play that is in hand when you mix with it things of an opposite nature, even though they are much better. Therefore go through with the play that is acting the best you can, and do not confound it because another that is pleasanter comes into your thoughts.

"It is even so in a commonwealth and in the councils of princes; if ill opinions cannot be quite rooted out, and you cannot cure some received vice according to your wishes, you must not, therefore, abandon the commonwealth, for the same reasons as you should not forsake the ship in a storm because you cannot command the winds. You are not obliged to assault people with discourses that are out of their road, when you see that their received notions must prevent your making an impression upon them: you ought rather to cast about and to manage things with all the dexterity in your power, so that, if you are not able to make them go well, they may be as little ill as possible; for, except all men were good, everything cannot be right, and that is a blessing that I do not at present hope to see."

"According to your argument," answered he, "all that I could be able to do would be to preserve myself from being mad while I endeavoured to cure the madness of others; for, if I speak with, I must repeat what I have said to you; and as for lying, whether a philosopher can do it or not I cannot tell: I am sure I cannot do it."

"But though these discourses may be uneasy and ungrateful to them, I do not see why they should seem foolish or extravagant; indeed, if I should either propose such things as Plato has contrived in his 'Commonwealth,' or as the Utopians practise in theirs, though they might seem better, as certainly they are, yet they are so different from our establishment, which is founded on property (there being no such thing among them), that I could not expect that it would have any effect on them. But such discourses as mine, which only call past evils to mind and give warning of what may follow, leave nothing in them that is so absurd that they may not be used at any time, for they can only be unpleasant to those who are resolved to run headlong the contrary way; and if we must let alone everything as absurd or extravagant–which, by reason of the wicked lives of many, may seem uncouth–we must, even among Christians, give over pressing the greatest part of those things that Christ hath taught us, though He has commanded us not to conceal them, but to proclaim on the housetops that which He taught in secret. The greatest parts of His precepts are more opposite to the lives of the men of this age than any part of my discourse has been, but the preachers seem to have learned that craft to which you advise me: for they, observing that the world would not willingly suit their lives to the rules that Christ has given, have fitted His doctrine, as if it had been a leaden rule, to their lives, that so, some way or other, they might agree with one another.

"But I see no other effect of this compliance except it be that men become more secure in their wickedness by it; and this is all the success that I can have in a court, for I must always differ from the rest, and then I shall signify nothing; or, if I agree with them, I shall then only help forward their madness. I do not comprehend what you mean by your 'casting about,' or by 'the bending and handling things so dexterously that, if they go not well, they may go as little ill as may be;' for in courts they will not bear with a man's holding his peace or conniving at what others do: a man must barefacedly approve of the worst counsels and consent to the blackest designs, so that he would pass for a spy, or, possibly, for a traitor, that did but coldly approve of such wicked practices; and therefore when a man is engaged in such a society, he will be so far from being able to mend matters by his 'casting about,' as you call it, that he will find no occasions of doing any good–the ill company will sooner corrupt him than be the better for him; or if, notwithstanding all their ill company, he still remains steady and innocent, yet their follies and knavery will be imputed to him; and, by mixing counsels with them, he must bear his share of all the blame that belongs wholly to others.

"It was no ill simile by which Plato set forth the unreasonableness of a philosopher's meddling with government. 'If a man,' says he, 'were to see a great company run out every day into the rain and take delight in being wet–if he knew that it would be to no purpose for him to go and persuade them to return to their houses in order to avoid the storm, and that all that could be expected by his going to speak to them would be that he himself should be as wet as they, it would be best for him to keep within doors, and, since he had not influence enough to correct other people's folly, to take care to preserve himself.'

"Though, to speak plainly my real sentiments, I must freely own that as long as there is any property, and while money is the standard of all other things, I cannot think that a nation can be governed either justly or happily: not justly, because the best things will fall to the share of the worst men; nor happily, because all things will be divided among a few (and even these are not in all respects happy), the rest being left to be absolutely miserable.

"Therefore, when I reflect on the wise and good constitution of the Utopians, among whom all things are so well governed and with so few laws, where virtue hath its due reward, and yet there is such an equality that every man lives in plenty–when I compare with them so many other nations that are still making new laws, and yet can never bring their constitution to a right regulation; where, notwithstanding every one has his property, yet all the laws that they can invent have not the power either to obtain or preserve it, or even to enable men certainly to distinguish what is their own from what is another's, of which the many lawsuits that every day break out, and are eternally depending, give too plain a demonstration–when, I say, I balance all these things in my thoughts, I grow more favourable to Plato, and do not wonder that he resolved not to make any laws for such as would not submit to a community of all things; for so wise a man could not but foresee that the setting all upon a level was the only way to make a nation happy; which cannot be obtained so long as there is property, for when every man draws to himself all that he can compass, by one title or another, it must needs follow that, how plentiful soever a nation may be, yet a few dividing the wealth of it among themselves, the rest must fall into indigence. So that there will be two sorts of people among them, who deserve that their fortunes should be interchanged–the former useless, but wicked and ravenous; and the latter, who by their constant industry serve the public more than themselves, sincere and modest men.

"From whence I am persuaded that till property is taken away, there can be no equitable or just distribution of things, nor can the world be happily governed; for as long as that is maintained, the greatest and the far best part of mankind, will be still oppressed with a load of cares and anxieties. I confess, without taking it quite away, those pressures that lie on a great part of mankind may be made lighter, but they can never be quite removed; for if laws were made to determine at how great an extent in soil, and at how much money, every man must stop–to limit the prince, that he might not grow too great; and to restrain the people, that they might not become too insolent–and that none might factiously aspire to public employments, which ought neither to be sold nor made burdensome by a great expense, since otherwise those that serve in them would be tempted to reimburse themselves by cheats and violence, and it would become necessary to find out rich men for undergoing those employments, which ought rather to be trusted to the wise. These laws, I say, might have such effect as good diet and care might have on a sick man whose recovery is desperate; they might allay and mitigate the disease, but it could never be quite healed, nor the body politic be brought again to a good habit as long as property remains; and it will fall out, as in a complication of diseases, that by applying a remedy to one sore you will provoke another, and that which removes the one ill symptom produces others, while the strengthening one part of the body weakens the rest."

"On the contrary," answered I, "it seems to me that men cannot live conveniently where all things are common. How can there be any plenty where every man will excuse himself from labour? for as the hope of gain doth not excite him, so the confidence that he has in other men's industry may make him slothful. If people come to be pinched with want, and yet cannot dispose of anything as their own, what can follow upon this but perpetual sedition and bloodshed, especially when the reverence and authority due to magistrates falls to the ground? for I cannot imagine how that can be kept up among those that are in all things equal to one another."

"I do not wonder," said he, "that it appears so to you, since you have no notion, or at least no right one, of such a constitution; but if you had been in Utopia with me, and had seen their laws and rules, as I did, for the space of five years, in which I lived among them, and during which time I was so delighted with them that indeed I should never have left them if it had not been to make the discovery of that new world to the Europeans, you would then confess that you had never seen a people so well constituted as they."

"You will not easily persuade me," said Peter, "that any nation in that new world is better governed than those among us; for as our understandings are not worse than theirs, so our government (if I mistake not) being more ancient, a long practice has helped us to find out many conveniences of life, and some happy chances have discovered other things to us which no man's understanding could ever have invented."

"As for the antiquity either of their government or of ours," said he, "you cannot pass a true judgment of it unless you had read their histories; for, if they are to be believed, they had towns among them before these parts were so much as inhabited; and as for those discoveries that have been either hit on by chance or made by ingenious men, these might have happened there as well as here. I do not deny but we are more ingenious than they are, but they exceed us much in industry and application. They knew little concerning us before our arrival among them. They call us all by a general name of 'The nations that lie beyond the equinoctial line' for their chronicle mentions a shipwreck that was made on their coast twelve hundred years ago, and that some Romans and Egyptians that were in the ship, getting safe ashore, spent the rest of their days amongst them; and such was their ingenuity that from this single opportunity they drew the advantage of learning from those unlooked-for guests, and acquired all the useful arts that were then among the Romans, and which were known to these shipwrecked men; and by the hints that they gave them they themselves found out even some of those arts which they could not fully explain, so happily did they improve that accident of having some of our people cast upon their shore. But if such an accident has at any time brought any from thence into Europe, we have been so far from improving it that we do not so much as remember it, as, in aftertimes perhaps, it will be forgot by our people that I was ever there; for though they, from one such accident, made themselves masters of all the good inventions that were among us, yet I believe it would be long before we should learn or put in practice any of the good institutions that are among them. And this is the true cause of their being better governed and living happier than we, though we come not short of them in point of understanding or outward advantages."

Upon this I said to him, "I earnestly beg you would describe that island very particularly to us; be not too short, but set out in order all things relating to their soil, their rivers, their towns, their people, their manners, constitution, laws, and, in a word, all that you imagine we desire to know; and you may well imagine that we desire to know everything concerning them of which we are hitherto ignorant."

"I will do it very willingly," said he, "for I have digested the whole matter carefully, but it will take up some time."

"Let us go, then," said I, "first and dine, and then we shall have leisure enough." He consented; we went in and dined, and after dinner came back and sat down in the same place. I ordered my servants to take care that none might come and interrupt us, and both Peter and I desired Raphael to be as good as his word. When he saw that we were very intent upon it he paused a little to recollect himself, and began in this manner:–

VI

BOOK TWO

"The island of Utopia is in the middle two hundred miles broad, and holds almost at the same breadth over a great part of it, but it grows narrower towards both ends. Its figure is not unlike a crescent. Between its horns the sea comes in eleven miles broad, and spreads itself into a great bay, which is environed with land to the compass of about five hundred miles, and is well secured from winds. In this bay there is no great current; the whole coast is, as it were, one continued harbour, which gives all that live in the island great convenience for mutual commerce. But the entry into the bay, occasioned by rocks on the one hand and shallows on the other, is very dangerous. In the middle of it there is one single rock which appears above water, and may, therefore, easily be avoided; and on the top of it there is a tower, in which a garrison is kept; the other rocks lie under water, and are very dangerous. The channel is known only to the natives; so that if any stranger should enter into the bay without one of their pilots he would run great danger of shipwreck. For even they themselves could not pass it safe if some marks that are on the coast did not direct their way; and if these should be but a little shifted, any fleet that might come against them, how great soever it were, would be certainly lost.

On the other side of the island there are likewise many harbours; and the coast is so fortified, both by nature and art, that a small number of men can hinder the descent of a great army. But they report (and there remains good marks of it to make it credible) that this was no island at first, but a part of the continent. Utopus, that conquered it (whose name it still carries, for Abraxa was its first name), brought the rude and uncivilised inhabitants into such a good government, and to that measure of politeness, that they now far excel all the rest of mankind. Having soon subdued them, he designed to separate them from the continent, and to bring the sea quite round them. To accomplish this he ordered a deep channel to be dug, fifteen miles long; and that the natives might not think he treated them like slaves, he not only forced the inhabitants, but also his own soldiers, to labour in carrying it on. As he set a vast number of men to work, he, beyond all men's expectations, brought it to a speedy conclusion. And his neighbours, who at first laughed at the folly of the undertaking, no sooner saw it brought to perfection than they were struck with admiration and terror.

There are fifty-four cities in the island, all large and well built, the manners, customs, and laws of which are the same, and they are all contrived as near in the same manner as the ground on which they stand will allow. The nearest lie at least twenty-four miles' distance from one another, and the most remote are not so far distant but that a man can go on foot in one day from it to that which lies next it.

Every city sends three of their wisest senators once a year to Amaurot, to consult about their common concerns; for that is the chief town of the island, being situated near the centre of it, so that it is the most convenient place for their assemblies. The jurisdiction of every city extends at least twenty miles, and, where the towns lie wider, they have much more ground. No town desires to enlarge its bounds, for the people consider themselves rather as tenants than landlords. They have built, over all the country, farmhouses for husbandmen, which are well contrived, and furnished with all things necessary for country labour. Inhabitants are sent, by turns, from the cities to dwell in them; no country family has fewer than forty men and women in it, besides two slaves. There is a master and a mistress set over every family, and over thirty families there is a magistrate. Every year twenty of this family come back to the town after they have stayed two years in the country, and in their room there are other twenty sent from the town, that they may learn country work from those that have been already one year in the country, as they must teach those that come to them the next from the town. By this means such as dwell in those country farms are never ignorant of agriculture, and so commit no errors which might otherwise be fatal and bring them under a scarcity of corn. But though there is every year such a shifting of the husbandmen to prevent any man being forced against his will to follow that hard course of life too long, yet many among them take such pleasure in it that they desire leave to continue in it many years.

These husbandmen till the ground, breed cattle, hew wood, and convey it to the towns either by land or water, as is most convenient. They breed an infinite multitude of chickens in a very curious manner; for the hens do not sit and hatch them, but a vast number of eggs are laid in a gentle and equal heat in order to be hatched, and they are no sooner out of the shell, and able to stir about, but they seem to consider those that feed them as their mothers, and follow them as other chickens do the hen that hatched them.

They breed very few horses, but those they have are full of mettle, and are kept only for exercising their youth in the art of sitting and riding them; for they do not put them to any work, either of ploughing or carriage, in which they employ oxen. For though their horses are stronger, yet they find oxen can hold out longer; and as they are not subject to so many diseases, so they are kept upon a less charge and with less trouble. And even when they are so worn out that they are no more fit for labour, they are good meat at last.

They sow no corn but that which is to be their bread; for they drink either wine, cider or perry, and often water, sometimes boiled with honey or liquorice, with which they abound; and though they know exactly how much corn will serve every town and all that tract of country which belongs to it, yet they sow much more and breed more cattle than are necessary for their consumption, and they give that overplus of which they make no use to their neighbours. When they want anything in the country which it does not produce, they fetch that from the town, without carrying anything in exchange for it. And the magistrates of the town take care to see it given them; for they meet generally in the town once a month, upon a festival day. When the time of harvest comes, the magistrates in the country send to those in the towns and let them know how many hands they will need for reaping the harvest; and the number they call for being sent to them, they commonly despatch it all in one day.

OF THEIR TOWNS, PARTICULARLY AMAUROT

He that knows one of their towns knows them all – they are so like one another, except where the situation makes some difference. I shall therefore describe one of them, and none is so proper as Amaurot; for as none is more eminent (all the rest yielding in precedence to this, because it is the seat of their supreme council), so there was none of them better known to me, I having lived five years all together in it.

It lies upon the side of a hill, or, rather, a rising ground. Its figure is almost square, for from the one side of it, which shoots up almost to the top of the hill, it runs down, in a descent for two miles, to the river Anider; but it is a little broader the other way that runs along by the bank of that river. The Anider rises about eighty miles above Amaurot, in a small spring at first. But other brooks falling into it, of which two are more considerable than the rest, as it runs by Amaurot it is grown half a mile broad; but, it still grows larger and larger, till, after sixty miles' course below it, it is lost in the ocean. Between the town and the sea, and for some miles above the town, it ebbs and flows every six hours with a strong current. The tide comes up about thirty miles so full that there is nothing but salt water in the river, the fresh water being driven back with its force; and above that, for some miles, the water is brackish; but a little higher, as it runs by the town, it is quite fresh; and when the tide ebbs, it continues fresh all along to the sea. There is a bridge cast over the river, not of timber, but of fair stone, consisting of many stately arches; it lies at that part of the town which is farthest from the sea, so that the ships, without any hindrance, lie all along the side of the town. There is, likewise, another river that runs by it, which, though it is not great, yet it runs pleasantly, for it rises out of the same hill on which the town stands, and so runs down through it and falls into the Anider.

The inhabitants have fortified the fountain-head of this river, which springs a little without the towns; that so, if they should happen to be besieged, the enemy might not be able to stop or divert the course of the water, nor poison it; from thence it is carried, in earthen pipes, to the lower streets. And for those places of the town to which the water of that small river cannot be conveyed, they have great cisterns for receiving the rain-water, which supplies the want of the other. The town is compassed with a high and thick wall, in which there are many towers and forts; there is also a broad and deep dry ditch, set thick with thorns, cast round three sides of the town, and the river is instead of a ditch on the fourth side. The streets are very convenient for all carriage, and are well sheltered from the winds.

Their buildings are good, and are so uniform that a whole side of a street looks like one house. The streets are twenty feet broad; there lie gardens behind all their houses. These are large, but enclosed with buildings, that on all hands face the streets, so that every house has both a door to the street and a back door to the garden. Their doors have all two leaves, which, as they are easily opened, so they shut of their own accord; and, there being no property among them, every man may freely enter into any house whatsoever.

At every ten years' end they shift their houses by lots. They cultivate their gardens with great care, so that they have both vines, fruits, herbs, and flowers in them; and all is so well ordered and so finely kept that I never saw gardens anywhere that were both so fruitful and so beautiful as theirs. And this humour of ordering their gardens so well is not only kept up by the pleasure they find in it, but also by an emulation between the inhabitants of the several streets, who vie with each other. And there is, indeed, nothing belonging to the whole town that is both more useful and more pleasant. So that he who founded the town seems to have taken care of nothing more than of their gardens; for they say the whole scheme of the town was designed at first by Utopus, but he left all that belonged to the ornament and improvement of it to be added by those that should come after him, that being too much for one man to bring to perfection.

Their records, that contain the history of their town and State, are preserved with an exact care, and run backwards seventeen hundred and sixty years. From these it appears that their houses were at first low and mean, like cottages, made of any sort of timber, and were built with mud walls and thatched with straw. But now their houses are three storeys high, the fronts of them are faced either with stone, plastering, or brick, and between the facings of their walls they throw in their rubbish. Their roofs are flat, and on them they lay a sort of plaster, which costs very little, and yet is so tempered that it is not apt to take fire, and yet resists the weather more than lead. They have great quantities of glass among them, with which they glaze their windows; they use also in their windows a thin linen cloth, that is so oiled or gummed that it both keeps out the wind and gives free admission to the light.

OF THEIR MAGISTRATES

Thirty families choose every year a magistrate, who was anciently called the Syphogrant, but is now called the Philarch; and over every ten Syphogrants, with the families subject to them, there is another magistrate, who was anciently called the Tranibore, but of late the Archphilarch. All the Syphogrants, who are in number two hundred, choose the Prince out of a list of four who are named by the people of the four divisions of the city; but they take an oath, before they proceed to an election, that they will choose him whom they think most fit for the office: they give him their voices secretly, so that it is not known for whom every one gives his suffrage. The Prince is for life, unless he is removed upon suspicion of some design to enslave the people. The Tranibors are new chosen every year, but yet they are, for the most part, continued; all their other magistrates are only annual.

The Tranibors meet every third day, and oftener if necessary, and consult with the Prince either concerning the affairs of the State in general, or such private differences as may arise sometimes among the people, though that falls out but seldom. There are always two Syphogrants called into the council chamber, and these are changed every day. It is a fundamental rule of their government, that no conclusion can be made in anything that relates to the public till it has been first debated three several days in their council. It is death for any to meet and consult concerning the State, unless it be either in their ordinary council, or in the assembly of the whole body of the people.

These things have been so provided among them that the Prince and the Tranibors may not conspire together to change the government and enslave the people; and therefore when anything of great importance is set on foot, it is sent to the Syphogrants, who, after they have communicated it to the families that belong to their divisions, and have considered it among themselves, make report to the senate; and, upon great occasions, the matter is referred to the council of the whole island. One rule observed in their council is, never to debate a thing on the same day in which it is first proposed; for that is always referred to the next meeting, that so men may not rashly and in the heat of discourse engage themselves too soon, which might bias them so much that, instead of consulting the good of the public, they might rather study to support their first opinions, and by a perverse and preposterous sort of shame hazard their country rather than endanger their own reputation, or venture the being suspected to have wanted foresight in the expedients that they at first proposed; and therefore, to prevent this, they take care that they may rather be deliberate than sudden in their motions.

OF THEIR TRADES, AND MANNER OF LIFE

Agriculture is that which is so universally understood among them that no person, either man or woman, is ignorant of it; they are instructed in it from their childhood, partly by what they learn at school, and partly by practice, they being led out often into the fields about the town, where they not only see others at work but are likewise exercised in it themselves.

Besides agriculture, which is so common to them all, every man has some peculiar trade to which he applies himself; such as the manufacture of wool or flax, masonry, smith's work, or carpenter's work; for there is no sort of trade that is in great esteem among them.

Throughout the island they wear the same sort of clothes, without any other distinction except what is necessary to distinguish the two sexes and the married and unmarried. The fashion never alters, and as it is neither disagreeable nor uneasy, so it is suited to the climate, and calculated both for their summers and winters. Every family makes their own clothes; but all among them, women as well as men, learn one or other of the trades formerly mentioned.

Women, for the most part, deal in wool and flax, which suit best with their weakness, leaving the ruder trades to the men. The same trade generally passes down from father to son, inclinations often following descent: but if any man's genius lies another way he is, by adoption, translated into a family that deals in the trade to which he is inclined; and when that is to be done, care is taken, not only by his father, but by the magistrate, that he may be put to a discreet and good man: and if, after a person has learned one trade, he desires to acquire another, that is also allowed, and is managed in the same manner as the former. When he has learned both, he follows that which he likes best, unless the public has more occasion for the other.

The chief, and almost the only, business of the Syphogrants is to take care that no man may live idle, but that every one may follow his trade diligently; yet they do not wear themselves out with perpetual toil from morning to night, as if they were beasts of burden, which as it is indeed a heavy slavery, so it is everywhere the common course of life amongst all mechanics except the Utopians: but they, dividing the day and night into twenty-four hours, appoint six of these for work, three of which are before dinner and three after; they then sup, and at eight o'clock, counting from noon, go to bed and sleep eight hours: the rest of their time, besides that taken up in work, eating, and sleeping, is left to every man's discretion; yet they are not to abuse that interval to luxury and idleness, but must employ it in some proper exercise, according to their various inclinations, which is, for the most part, reading.

It is ordinary to have public lectures every morning before daybreak, at which none are obliged to appear but those who are marked out for literature; yet a great many, both men and women, of all ranks, go to hear lectures of one sort or other, according to their inclinations: but if others that are not made for contemplation, choose rather to employ themselves at that time in their trades, as many of them do, they are not hindered, but are rather commended, as men that take care to serve their country.

After supper they spend an hour in some diversion, in summer in their gardens, and in winter in the halls where they eat, where they entertain each other either with music or discourse. They do not so much as know dice, or any such foolish and mischievous games. They have, however, two sorts of games not unlike our chess; the one is between several numbers, in which one number, as it were, consumes another; the other resembles a battle between the virtues and the vices, in which the enmity in the vices among themselves, and their agreement against virtue, is not unpleasantly represented; together with the special opposition between the particular virtues and vices; as also the methods by which vice either openly assaults or secretly undermines virtue; and virtue, on the other hand, resists it.

But the time appointed for labour is to be narrowly examined, otherwise you may imagine that since there are only six hours appointed for work, they may fall under a scarcity of necessary provisions: but it is so far from being true that this time is not sufficient for supplying them with plenty of all things, either necessary or convenient, that it is rather too much; and this you will easily apprehend if you consider how great a part of all other nations is quite idle.

First, women generally do little, who are the half of mankind; and if some few women are diligent, their husbands are idle: then consider the great company of idle priests, and of those that are called religious men; add to these all rich men, chiefly those that have estates in land, who are called noblemen and gentlemen, together with their families, made up of idle persons, that are kept more for show than use; add to these all those strong and lusty beggars that go about pretending some disease in excuse for their begging;

and upon the whole account you will find that the number of those by whose labours mankind is supplied is much less than you perhaps imagined: then consider how few of those that work are employed in labours that are of real service, for we, who measure all things by money, give rise to many trades that are both vain and superfluous, and serve only to support riot and luxury: for if those who work were employed only in such things as the conveniences of life require, there would be such an abundance of them that the prices of them would so sink that tradesmen could not be maintained by their gains; if all those who labour about useless things were set to more profitable employments, and if all they that languish out their lives in sloth and idleness (every one of whom consumes as much as any two of the men that are at work) were forced to labour, you may easily imagine that a small proportion of time would serve for doing all that is either necessary, profitable, or pleasant to mankind, especially while pleasure is kept within its due bounds: this appears very plainly in Utopia; for there, in a great city, and in all the territory that lies round it, you can scarce find five hundred, either men or women, by their age and strength capable of labour, that are not engaged in it.

Even the Syphogrants, though excused by the law, yet do not excuse themselves, but work, that by their examples they may excite the industry of the rest of the people; the like exemption is allowed to those who, being recommended to the people by the priests, are, by the secret suffrages of the Syphogrants, privileged from labour, that they may apply themselves wholly to study; and if any of these fall short of those hopes that they seemed at first to give, they are obliged to return to work; and sometimes a mechanic that so employs his leisure hours as to make a considerable advancement in learning is eased from being a tradesman and ranked among their learned men. Out of these they choose their ambassadors, their priests, their Tranibors, and the Prince himself, anciently called their Barzenes, but is called of late their Ademus.

And thus from the great numbers among them that are neither suffered to be idle nor to be employed in any fruitless labour, you may easily make the estimate how much may be done in those few hours in which they are obliged to labour. But, besides all that has been already said, it is to be considered that the needful arts among them are managed with less labour than anywhere else. The building or the repairing of houses among us employ many hands, because often a thriftless heir suffers a house that his father built to fall into decay, so that his successor must, at a great cost, repair that which he might have kept up with a small charge; it frequently happens that the same house which one person built at a vast expense is neglected by another, who thinks he has a more delicate sense of the beauties of architecture, and he, suffering it to fall to ruin, builds another at no less charge. But among the Utopians all things are so regulated that men very seldom build upon a new piece of ground, and are not only very quick in repairing their houses, but show their foresight in preventing their decay, so that their buildings are preserved very long with but very little labour, and thus the builders, to whom that care belongs, are often without employment, except the hewing of timber and the squaring of stones, that the materials may be in readiness for raising a building very suddenly when there is any occasion for it.

As to their clothes, observe how little work is spent in them; while they are at labour they are clothed with leather and skins, cut carelessly about them, which will last seven years, and when they appear in public they put on an upper garment which hides the other; and these are all of one colour, and that is the natural colour of the wool. As they need less woollen cloth than is used anywhere else, so that which they make use of is much less costly; they use linen cloth more, but that is prepared with less labour, and they value cloth only by the whiteness of the linen or the cleanness of the wool, without much regard to the fineness of the thread. While in other places four or five upper garments of woollen cloth of different colours, and as many vests of silk, will scarce serve one man, and while those that are nicer think ten too few, every man there is content with one, which very often serves him two years; nor is there anything that can tempt a man to desire more, for if he had them he would neither be the, warmer nor would he make one jot the better appearance for it.

And thus, since they are all employed in some useful labour, and since they content themselves with fewer things, it falls out that there is a great abundance of all things among them; so that it frequently happens that, for want of other work, vast numbers are sent out to mend the highways; but when no public undertaking is to be performed, the hours of working are lessened. The magistrates never engage the people in unnecessary labour, since the chief end of the constitution is to regulate labour by the necessities of the public, and to allow the people as much time as is necessary for the improvement of their minds, in which they think the happiness of life consists.

OF THEIR SOCIAL RELATIONS

But it is now time to explain to you the mutual intercourse of this people, their commerce, and the rules by which all things are distributed among them.

As their cities are composed of families, so their families are made up of those that are nearly related to one another. Their women, when they grow up, are married out, but all the males, both children and grand-children, live still in the same house, in great obedience to their common parent, unless age has weakened his understanding, and in that case he that is next to him in age comes in his room; but lest any city should become either too great, or by any accident be dispeopled, provision is made that none of their cities may contain above six thousand families, besides those of the country around it. No family may have less than ten and more than sixteen persons in it, but there can be no determined number for the children under age; this rule is easily observed by removing some of the children of a more fruitful couple to any other family that does not abound so much in them.

By the same rule they supply cities that do not increase so fast from others that breed faster; and if there is any increase over the whole island, then they draw out a number of their citizens out of the several towns and send them over to the neighbouring continent, where, if they find that the inhabitants have more soil than they can well cultivate, they fix a colony, taking the inhabitants into their society if they are willing to live with them; and where they do that of their own accord, they quickly enter into their method of life and conform to their rules, and this proves a happiness to both nations; for, according to their constitution, such care is taken of the soil that it becomes fruitful enough for both, though it might be otherwise too narrow and barren for any one of them.

But if the natives refuse to conform themselves to their laws they drive them out of those bounds which they mark out for themselves, and use force if they resist, for they account it a very just cause of war for a nation to hinder others from possessing a part of that soil of which they make no use, but which is suffered to lie idle and uncultivated, since every man has, by the law of nature, a right to such a waste portion of the earth as is necessary for his subsistence. If an accident has so lessened the number of the inhabitants of any of their towns that it cannot be made up from the other towns of the island without diminishing them too much (which is said to have fallen out but twice since they were first a people, when great numbers were carried off by the plague), the loss is then supplied by recalling as many as are wanted from their colonies, for they will abandon these rather than suffer the towns in the island to sink too low.

But to return to their manner of living in society: the oldest man of every family, as has been already said, is its governor; wives serve their husbands, and children their parents, and always the younger serves the elder.

BOOK TWO

Every city is divided into four equal parts, and in the middle of each there is a market-place. What is brought thither, and manufactured by the several families, is carried from thence to houses appointed for that purpose, in which all things of a sort are laid by themselves; and thither every father goes, and takes whatsoever he or his family stand in need of, without either paying for it or leaving anything in exchange. There is no reason for giving a denial to any person, since there is such plenty of everything among them; and there is no danger of a man's asking for more than he needs; they have no inducements to do this, since they are sure they shall always be supplied: it is the fear of want that makes any of the whole race of animals either greedy or ravenous; but, besides fear, there is in man a pride that makes him fancy it a particular glory to excel others in pomp and excess; but by the laws of the Utopians, there is no room for this.

Near these markets there are others for all sorts of provisions, where there are not only herbs, fruits, and bread, but also fish, fowl, and cattle. There are also, without their towns, places appointed near some running water for killing their beasts and for washing away their filth, which is done by their slaves; for they suffer none of their citizens to kill their cattle, because they think that pity and good-nature, which are among the best of those affections that are born with us, are much impaired by the butchering of animals; nor do they suffer anything that is foul or unclean to be brought within their towns, lest the air should be infected by ill-smells, which might prejudice their health.

In every street there are great halls, that lie at an equal distance from each other, distinguished by particular names. The Syphogrants dwell in those that are set over thirty families, fifteen lying on one side of it, and as many on the other. In these halls they all meet and have their repasts; the stewards of every one of them come to the market-place at an appointed hour, and according to the number of those that belong to the hall they carry home provisions.

But they take more care of their sick than of any others; these are lodged and provided for in public hospitals. They have belonging to every town four hospitals, that are built without their walls, and are so large that they may pass for little towns; by this means, if they had ever such a number of sick persons, they could lodge them conveniently, and at such a distance that such of them as are sick of infectious diseases may be kept so far from the rest that there can be no danger of contagion. The hospitals are furnished and stored with all things that are convenient for the ease and recovery of the sick;

and those that are put in them are looked after with such tender and watchful care, and are so constantly attended by their skilful physicians, that as none is sent to them against their will, so there is scarce one in a whole town that, if he should fall ill, would not choose rather to go thither than lie sick at home.

After the steward of the hospitals has taken for the sick whatsoever the physician prescribes, then the best things that are left in the market are distributed equally among the halls in proportion to their numbers; only, in the first place, they serve the Prince, the Chief Priest, the Tranibors, the Ambassadors, and strangers, if there are any, which, indeed, falls out but seldom, and for whom there are houses, well furnished, particularly appointed for their reception when they come among them. At the hours of dinner and supper the whole Syphogranty being called together by sound of trumpet, they meet and eat together, except only such as are in the hospitals or lie sick at home. Yet, after the halls are served, no man is hindered to carry provisions home from the market-place, for they know that none does that but for some good reason; for though any that will may eat at home, yet none does it willingly, since it is both ridiculous and foolish for any to give themselves the trouble to make ready an ill dinner at home when there is a much more plentiful one made ready for him so near hand. All the uneasy and sordid services about these halls are performed by their slaves; but the dressing and cooking their meat, and the ordering their tables, belong only to the women, all those of every family taking it by turns.

They sit at three or more tables, according to their number; the men sit towards the wall, and the women sit on the other side, that if any of them should be taken suddenly ill, which is no uncommon case amongst women with child, she may, without disturbing the rest, rise and go to the nurses' room (who are there with the sucking children), where there is always clean water at hand and cradles, in which they may lay the young children if there is occasion for it, and a fire, that they may shift and dress them before it. Every child is nursed by its own mother if death or sickness does not intervene; and in that case the Syphogrants' wives find out a nurse quickly, which is no hard matter, for any one that can do it offers herself cheerfully; for as they are much inclined to that piece of mercy, so the child whom they nurse considers the nurse as its mother. All the children under five years old sit among the nurses; the rest of the younger sort of both sexes, till they are fit for marriage, either serve those that sit at table, or, if they are not strong enough for that, stand by them in great silence and eat what is given them; nor have they any other formality of dining.

In the middle of the first table, which stands across the upper end of the hall, sit the Syphogrant and his wife, for that is the chief and most conspicuous place; next to him sit two of the most ancient, for there go always four to a mess. If there is a temple within the Syphogranty, the Priest and his wife sit with the Syphogrant above all the rest; next them there is a mixture of old and young, who are so placed that as the young are set near others, so they are mixed with the more ancient; which, they say, was appointed on this account: that the gravity of the old people, and the reverence that is due to them, might restrain the younger from all indecent words and gestures. Dishes are not served up to the whole table at first, but the best are first set before the old, whose seats are distinguished from the young, and, after them, all the rest are served alike. The old men distribute to the younger any curious meats that happen to be set before them, if there is not such an abundance of them that the whole company may be served alike.

Thus old men are honoured with a particular respect, yet all the rest fare as well as they. Both dinner and supper are begun with some lecture of morality that is read to them; but it is so short that it is not tedious nor uneasy to them to hear it. From hence the old men take occasion to entertain those about them with some useful and pleasant enlargements; but they do not engross the whole discourse so to themselves during their meals that the younger may not put in for a share; on the contrary, they engage them to talk, that so they may, in that free way of conversation, find out the force of every one's spirit and observe his temper.

They despatch their dinners quickly, but sit long at supper, because they go to work after the one, and are to sleep after the other, during which they think the stomach carries on the concoction more vigorously. They never sup without music, and there is always fruit served up after meat; while they are at table some burn perfumes and sprinkle about fragrant ointments and sweet waters—in short, they want nothing that may cheer up their spirits; they give themselves a large allowance that way, and indulge themselves in all such pleasures as are attended with no inconvenience.

Thus do those that are in the towns live together; but in the country, where they live at a great distance, every one eats at home, and no family wants any necessary sort of provision, for it is from them that provisions are sent unto those that live in the towns.

OF THE TRAVEL OF THE UTOPIANS

If any man has a mind to visit his friends that live in some other town, or desires to travel and see the rest of the country, he obtains leave very easily from the Syphogrant and Tranibors, when there is no particular occasion for him at home. Such as travel carry with them a passport from the Prince, which both certifies the licence that is granted for travelling, and limits the time of their return. They are furnished with a waggon and a slave, who drives the oxen and looks after them; but, unless there are women in the company, the waggon is sent back at the end of the journey as a needless encumbrance. While they are on the road they carry no provisions with them, yet they want for nothing, but are everywhere treated as if they were at home. If they stay in any place longer than a night, every one follows his proper occupation, and is very well used by those of his own trade; but if any man goes out of the city to which he belongs without leave, and is found rambling without a passport, he is severely treated, he is punished as a fugitive, and sent home disgracefully; and, if he falls again into the like fault, is condemned to slavery.

If any man has a mind to travel only over the precinct of his own city, he may freely do it, with his father's permission and his wife's consent; but when he comes into any of the country houses, if he expects to be entertained by them, he must labour with them and conform to their rules; and if he does this, he may freely go over the whole precinct, being then as useful to the city to which he belongs as if he were still within it. Thus you see that there are no idle persons among them, nor pretences of excusing any from labour. There are no taverns, no ale-houses, nor stews among them, nor any other occasions of corrupting each other, of getting into corners, or forming themselves into parties; all men live in full view, so that all are obliged both to perform their ordinary task and to employ themselves well in their spare hours; and it is certain that a people thus ordered must live in great abundance of all things, and these being equally distributed among them, no man can want or be obliged to beg.

In their great council at Amaurot, to which there are three sent from every town once a year, they examine what towns abound in provisions and what are under any scarcity, that so the one may be furnished from the other; and this is done freely, without any sort of exchange; for, according to their plenty or scarcity, they supply or are supplied from one another, so that indeed the whole island is, as it were, one family.

OF THEIR WEALTH

When they have thus taken care of their whole country, and laid up stores for two years (which they do to prevent the ill consequences of an unfavourable season), they order an exportation of the overplus, both of corn, honey, wool, flax, wood, wax, tallow, leather, and cattle, which they send out, commonly in great quantities, to other nations. They order a seventh part of all these goods to be freely given to the poor of the countries to which they send them, and sell the rest at moderate rates; and by this exchange they not only bring back those few things that they need at home (for, indeed, they scarce need anything but iron), but likewise a great deal of gold and silver; and by their driving this trade so long, it is not to be imagined how vast a treasure they have got among them, so that now they do not much care whether they sell off their merchandise for money in hand or upon trust.

A great part of their treasure is now in bonds; but in all their contracts no private man stands bound, but the writing runs in the name of the town; and the towns that owe them money raise it from those private hands that owe it to them, lay it up in their public chamber, or enjoy the profit of it till the Utopians call for it; and they choose rather to let the greatest part of it lie in their hands, who make advantage by it, than to call for it themselves; but if they see that any of their other neighbours stand more in need of it, then they call it in and lend it to them.

Whenever they are engaged in war, which is the only occasion in which their treasure can be usefully employed, they make use of it themselves; in great extremities or sudden accidents they employ it in hiring foreign troops, whom they more willingly expose to danger than their own people; they give them great pay, knowing well that this will work even on their enemies; that it will engage them either to betray their own side, or, at least, to desert it; and that it is the best means of raising mutual jealousies among them. For this end they have an incredible treasure; but they do not keep it as a treasure, but in such a manner as I am almost afraid to tell, lest you think it so extravagant as to be hardly credible. This I have the more reason to apprehend because, if I had not seen it myself, I could not have been easily persuaded to have believed it upon any man's report.

It is certain that all things appear incredible to us in proportion as they differ from known customs; but one who can judge aright will not wonder to find that, since their constitution differs so much from ours, their value of gold and silver should be measured by a very different standard; for since they have no use for money among themselves, but keep it as a provision against events which seldom happen, and between which there are generally long intervening intervals, they value it no farther than it deserves–that is, in proportion to its use. So that it is plain they must prefer iron either to gold or silver, for men can no more live without iron than without fire or water; but Nature has marked out no use for the other metals so essential as not easily to be dispensed with. The folly of men has enhanced the value of gold and silver because of their scarcity; whereas, on the contrary, it is their opinion that Nature, as an indulgent parent, has freely given us all the best things in great abundance, such as water and earth, but has laid up and hid from us the things that are vain and useless.

If these metals were laid up in any tower in the kingdom it would raise a jealousy of the Prince and Senate, and give birth to that foolish mistrust into which the people are apt to fall–a jealousy of their intending to sacrifice the interest of the public to their own private advantage. If they should work it into vessels, or any sort of plate, they fear that the people might grow too fond of it, and so be unwilling to let the plate be run down, if a war made it necessary, to employ it in paying their soldiers.

To prevent all these inconveniences they have fallen upon an expedient which, as it agrees with their other policy, so is it very different from ours, and will scarce gain belief among us who value gold so much, and lay it up so carefully. They eat and drink out of vessels of earth or glass, which make an agreeable appearance, though formed of brittle materials; while they make their chamber-pots and close- stools of gold and silver, and that not only in their public halls but in their private houses. Of the same metals they likewise make chains and fetters for their slaves, to some of which, as a badge of infamy, they hang an earring of gold, and make others wear a chain or a coronet of the same metal; and thus they take care by all possible means to render gold and silver of no esteem; and from hence it is that while other nations part with their gold and silver as unwillingly as if one tore out their bowels, those of Utopia would look on their giving in all they possess of those metals (when there were any use for them) but as the parting with a trifle, or as we would esteem the loss of a penny!

They find pearls on their coasts, and diamonds and carbuncles on their rocks; they do not look after them, but, if they find them by chance, they polish them, and with them they adorn their children, who are delighted with them, and glory in them during their childhood; but when they grow to years, and see that none but children use such baubles, they of their own accord, without being bid by their parents, lay them aside, and would be as much ashamed to use them afterwards as children among us, when they come to years, are of their puppets and other toys.

I never saw a clearer instance of the opposite impressions that different customs make on people than I observed in the ambassadors of the Anemolians, who came to Amaurot when I was there. As they came to treat of affairs of great consequence, the deputies from several towns met together to wait for their coming. The ambassadors of the nations that lie near Utopia, knowing their customs, and that fine clothes are in no esteem among them, that silk is despised, and gold is a badge of infamy, used to come very modestly clothed; but the Anemolians, lying more remote, and having had little commerce with them, understanding that they were coarsely clothed, and all in the same manner, took it for granted that they had none of those fine things among them of which they made no use; and they, being a vainglorious rather than a wise people, resolved to set themselves out with so much pomp that they should look like gods, and strike the eyes of the poor Utopians with their splendour.

Thus three ambassadors made their entry with a hundred attendants, all clad in garments of different colours, and the greater part in silk; the ambassadors themselves, who were of the nobility of their country, were in cloth-of-gold, and adorned with massy chains, earrings and rings of gold; their caps were covered with bracelets set full of pearls and other gems–in a word, they were set out with all those things that among the Utopians were either the badges of slavery, the marks of infamy, or the playthings of children. It was not unpleasant to see, on the one side, how they looked big, when they compared their rich habits with the plain clothes of the Utopians, who were come out in great numbers to see them make their entry; and, on the other, to observe how much they were mistaken in the impression which they hoped this pomp would have made on them. It appeared so ridiculous a show to all that had never stirred out of their country, and had not seen the customs of other nations, that though they paid some reverence to those that were the most meanly clad, as if they had been the ambassadors, yet when they saw the ambassadors themselves so full of gold and chains, they looked upon them as slaves, and forbore to treat them with reverence.

You might have seen the children who were grown big enough to despise their playthings, and who had thrown away their jewels, call to their mothers, push them gently, and cry out, 'See that great fool, that wears pearls and gems as if he were yet a child!' while their mothers very innocently replied, 'Hold your peace! this, I believe, is one of the ambassadors' fools.' Others censured the fashion of their chains, and observed, 'That they were of no use, for they were too slight to bind their slaves, who could easily break them; and, besides, hung so loose about them that they thought it easy to throw their away, and so get from them.

But after the ambassadors had stayed a day among them, and saw so vast a quantity of gold in their houses (which was as much despised by them as it was esteemed in other nations), and beheld more gold and silver in the chains and fetters of one slave than all their ornaments amounted to, their plumes fell, and they were ashamed of all that glory for which they had formed valued themselves, and accordingly laid it aside–a resolution that they immediately took when, on their engaging in some free discourse with the Utopians, they discovered their sense of such things and their other customs.

The Utopians wonder how any man should be so much taken with the glaring doubtful lustre of a jewel or a stone, that can look up to a star or to the sun himself; or how any should value himself because his cloth is made of a finer thread; for, how fine soever that thread may be, it was once no better than the fleece of a sheep, and that sheep, was a sheep still, for all its wearing it. They wonder much to hear that gold, which in itself is so useless a thing, should be everywhere so much esteemed that even man, for whom it was made, and by whom it has its value, should yet be thought of less value than this metal; that a man of lead, who has no more sense than a log of wood, and is as bad as he is foolish, should have many wise and good men to serve him, only because he has a great heap of that metal; and that if it should happen that by some accident or trick of law (which, sometimes produces as great changes as chance itself) all this wealth should pass from the master to the meanest varlet of his whole family, he himself would very soon become one of his servants, as if he were a thing that belonged to his wealth, and so were bound to follow its fortune! But they much more admire and detest the folly of those who, when they see a rich man, though they neither owe him anything, nor are in any sort dependent on his bounty, yet, merely because he is rich, give him little less than divine honours, even though they know him to be so covetous and base-minded that, notwithstanding all his wealth, he will not part with one farthing of it to them as long as he lives!

OF THEIR LEARNING AND PHILOSOPHIES

These and such like notions have that people imbibed, partly from their education, being bred in a country whose customs and laws are opposite to all such foolish maxims, and partly from their learning and studies–for though there are but few in any town that are so wholly excused from labour as to give themselves entirely up to their studies (these being only such persons as discover from their childhood an extraordinary capacity and disposition for letters), yet their children and a great part of the nation, both men and women, are taught to spend those hours in which they are not obliged to work in reading; and this they do through the whole progress of life.

They have all their learning in their own tongue, which is both a copious and pleasant language, and in which a man can fully express his mind; it runs over a great tract of many countries, but it is not equally pure in all places. They had never so much as heard of the names of any of those philosophers that are so famous in these parts of the world, before we went among them; and yet they had made the same discoveries as the Greeks, both in music, logic, arithmetic, and geometry.

But as they are almost in everything equal to the ancient philosophers, so they far exceed our modern logicians for they have never yet fallen upon the barbarous niceties that our youth are forced to learn in those trifling logical schools that are among us. They are so far from minding chimeras and fantastical images made in the mind that none of them could comprehend what we meant when we talked to them of a man in the abstract as common to all men in particular (so that though we spoke of him as a thing that we could point at with our fingers, yet none of them could perceive him) and yet distinct from every one, as if he were some monstrous Colossus or giant; yet, for all this ignorance of these empty notions, they knew astronomy, and were perfectly acquainted with the motions of the heavenly bodies; and have many instruments, well contrived and divided, by which they very accurately compute the course and positions of the sun, moon, and stars. But for the cheat of divining by the stars, by their oppositions or conjunctions, it has not so much as entered into their thoughts.

They have a particular sagacity, founded upon much observation, in judging of the weather, by which they know when they may look for rain, wind, or other alterations in the air; but as to the philosophy of these things, the cause of the saltness of the sea, of its ebbing and flowing, and of the original and nature both of the heavens and the earth, they dispute of them partly as our ancient philosophers have done, and partly upon some new hypothesis, in which, as they differ from them, so they do not in all things agree among themselves.

As to moral philosophy, they have the same disputes among them as we have here. They examine what are properly good, both for the body and the mind; and whether any outward thing can be called truly *good*, or if that term belong only to the endowments of the soul. They inquire, likewise, into the nature of virtue and pleasure. But their chief dispute is concerning the happiness of a man, and wherein it consists—whether in some one thing or in a great many. They seem, indeed, more inclinable to that opinion that places, if not the whole, yet the chief part, of a man's happiness in pleasure; and, what may seem more strange, they make use of arguments even from religion, notwithstanding its severity and roughness, for the support of that opinion so indulgent to pleasure; for they never dispute concerning happiness without fetching some arguments from the principles of religion as well as from natural reason, since without the former they reckon that all our inquiries after happiness must be but conjectural and defective.

These are their religious principles:–That the soul of man is immortal, and that God of His goodness has designed that it should be happy; and that He has, therefore, appointed rewards for good and virtuous actions, and punishments for vice, to be distributed after this life.

Though these principles of religion are conveyed down among them by tradition, they think that even reason itself determines a man to believe and acknowledge them; and freely confess that if these were taken away, no man would be so insensible as not to seek after pleasure by all possible means, lawful or unlawful, using only this caution–that a lesser pleasure might not stand in the way of a greater, and that no pleasure ought to be pursued that should draw a great deal of pain after it; for they think it the maddest thing in the world to pursue virtue, that is a sour and difficult thing, and not only to renounce the pleasures of life, but willingly to undergo much pain and trouble, if a man has no prospect of a reward. And what reward can there be for one that has passed his whole life, not only without pleasure, but in pain, if there is nothing to be expected after death? Yet they do not place happiness in all sorts of pleasures, but only in those that in themselves are good and honest.

There is a party among them who place happiness in bare virtue; others think that our natures are conducted by virtue to happiness, as that which is the chief good of man. They define virtue thus–that it is a living according to Nature, and think that we are made by God for that end; they believe that a man then follows the dictates of Nature when he pursues or avoids things according to the direction of reason. They say that the first dictate of reason is the kindling in us a love and reverence for the Divine Majesty, to whom we owe both all that we have and, all that we can ever hope for. In the next place, reason directs us to keep our minds as free from passion and as cheerful as we can, and that we should consider ourselves as bound by the ties of good-nature and humanity to use our utmost endeavours to help forward the happiness of all other persons; for there never was any man such a morose and severe pursuer of virtue, such an enemy to pleasure, that though he set hard rules for men to undergo, much pain, many watchings, and other rigors, yet did not at the same time advise them to do all they could in order to relieve and ease the miserable, and who did not represent gentleness and good-nature as amiable dispositions. And from thence they infer that if a man ought to advance the welfare and comfort of the rest of mankind (there being no virtue more proper and peculiar to our nature than to ease the miseries of others, to free from trouble and anxiety, in furnishing them with the comforts of life, in which pleasure consists.)

Nature much more vigorously leads them to do all this for himself. A life of pleasure is either a real evil, and in that case we ought not to assist others in their pursuit of it, but, on the contrary, to keep them from it all we can, as from that which is most hurtful and deadly; or if it is a good thing, so that we not only may but ought to help others to it, why, then, ought not a man to begin with himself? Since no man can be more bound to look after the good of another than after his own; for Nature cannot direct us to be good and kind to others, and yet at the same time to be unmerciful and cruel to ourselves. Thus as they define virtue to be living according to Nature, so they imagine that Nature prompts all people on to seek after pleasure as the end of all they do.

They also observe that in order to our supporting the pleasures of life, Nature inclines us to enter into society; for there is no man so much raised above the rest of mankind as to be the only favourite of Nature, who, on the contrary, seems to have placed on a level all those that belong to the same species. Upon this they infer that no man ought to seek his own conveniences so eagerly as to prejudice others;

and therefore they think that not only all agreements between private persons ought to be observed, but likewise that all those laws ought to be kept which either a good prince has published in due form, or to which a people that is neither oppressed with tyranny nor circumvented by fraud has consented, for distributing those conveniences of life which afford us all our pleasures.

They think it is an evidence of true wisdom for a man to pursue his own advantage as far as the laws allow it, they account it piety to prefer the public good to one's private concerns, but they think it unjust for a man to seek for pleasure by snatching another man's pleasures from him; and, on the contrary, they think it a sign of a gentle and good soul for a man to dispense with his own advantage for the good of others, and that by this means a good man finds as much pleasure one way as he parts with another; for as he may expect the like from others when he may come to need it, so, if that should fail him, yet the sense of a good action, and the reflections that he makes on the love and gratitude of those whom he has so obliged, gives the mind more pleasure than the body could have found in that from which it had restrained itself. They are also persuaded that God will make up the loss of those small pleasures with a vast and endless joy, of which religion easily convinces a good soul.

Thus, upon an inquiry into the whole matter, they reckon that all our actions, and even all our virtues, terminate in pleasure, as in our chief end and greatest happiness; and they call every motion or state, either of body or mind, in which Nature teaches us to delight, a pleasure. Thus they cautiously limit pleasure only to those appetites to which Nature leads us; for they say that Nature leads us only to those delights to which reason, as well as sense, carries us, and by which we neither injure any other person nor lose the possession of greater pleasures, and of such as draw no troubles after them. But they look upon those delights which men by a foolish, though common, mistake call pleasure, as if they could change as easily the nature of things as the use of words, as things that greatly obstruct their real happiness, instead of advancing it, because they so entirely possess the minds of those that are once captivated by them with a false notion of pleasure that there is no room left for pleasures of a truer or purer kind.

There are many things that in themselves have nothing that is truly delightful; on the contrary, they have a good deal of bitterness in them; and yet, from our perverse appetites after forbidden objects, are not only ranked among the pleasures, but are made even the greatest designs, of life. Among those who pursue these sophisticated pleasures they reckon such as I mentioned before, who think themselves really the better for having fine clothes; in which they think they are doubly mistaken, both in the opinion they have of their clothes, and in that they have of themselves. For if you consider the use of clothes, why should a fine thread be thought better than a coarse one? And yet these men, as if they had some real advantages beyond others, and did not owe them wholly to their mistakes, look big, seem to fancy themselves to be more valuable, and imagine that a respect is due to them for the sake of a rich garment, to which they would not have pretended if they had been more meanly clothed, and even resent it as an affront if that respect is not paid them.

It is also a great folly to be taken with outward marks of respect, which signify nothing; for what true or real pleasure can one man find in another's standing bare or making legs to him? Will the bending another man's knees give ease to yours? And will the head's being bare cure the madness of yours? And yet it is wonderful to see how this false notion of pleasure bewitches many who delight themselves with the fancy of their nobility, and are pleased with this conceit–that they are descended from ancestors who have been held for some successions rich, and who have had great possessions; for this is all that makes nobility at present. Yet they do not think themselves a whit the less noble, though their immediate parents have left none of this wealth to them, or though they themselves have squandered it away.

The Utopians have no better opinion of those who are much taken with gems and precious stones, and who account it a degree of happiness next to a divine one if they can purchase one that is very extraordinary, especially if it be of that sort of stones that is then in greatest request, for the same sort is not at all times universally of the same value, nor will men buy it unless it be dismounted and taken out of the gold. The jeweller is then made to give good security, and required solemnly to swear that the stone is true, that, by such an exact caution, a false one might not be bought instead of a true; though, if you were to examine it, your eye could find no difference between the counterfeit and that which is true; so that they are all one to you, as much as if you were blind. Or can it be thought that they who heap up a useless mass of wealth, not for any use that it is to bring them, but merely to please themselves with the contemplation of it, enjoy any true pleasure in it? The delight they find is only a false shadow of joy. Those are no better whose error is somewhat different from the former, and who hide it out of their fear of losing it; for what other name can fit the hiding it in the earth, or, rather, the restoring it to it again, it being thus cut off from being useful either to its owner or to the rest of mankind? And yet the owner, having hid it carefully, is glad, because he thinks he is now sure of it. If it should be stole, the owner, though he might live perhaps ten years after the theft, of which he knew nothing, would find no difference between his having or losing it, for both ways it was equally useless to him.

Among those foolish pursuers of pleasure they reckon all that delight in hunting, in fowling, or gaming, of whose madness they have only heard, for they have no such things among them. But they have asked us, 'What sort of pleasure is it that men can find in throwing the dice?' (for if there were any pleasure in it, they think the doing it so often should give one a surfeit of it); 'and what pleasure can one find in hearing the barking and howling of dogs, which seem rather odious than pleasant sounds?' Nor can they comprehend the pleasure of seeing dogs run after a hare, more than of seeing one dog run after another; for if the seeing them run is that which gives the pleasure, you have the same entertainment to the eye on both these occasions, since that is the same in both cases. But if the pleasure lies in seeing the hare killed and torn by the dogs, this ought rather to stir pity, that a weak, harmless, and fearful hare should be devoured by strong, fierce, and cruel dogs. Therefore all this business of hunting is, among the Utopians, turned over to their butchers, and those, as has been already said, are all slaves, and they look on hunting as one of the basest parts of a butcher's work, for they account it both more profitable and more decent to kill those beasts that are more necessary and useful to mankind, whereas the killing and tearing of so small and miserable an animal can only attract the huntsman with a false show of pleasure, from which he can reap but small advantage. They look on the desire of the bloodshed, even of beasts, as a mark of a mind that is already corrupted with cruelty, or that at least, by too frequent returns of so brutal a pleasure, must degenerate into it.

Thus though the rabble of mankind look upon these, and on innumerable other things of the same nature, as pleasures, the Utopians, on the contrary, observing that there is nothing in them truly pleasant, conclude that they are not to be reckoned among pleasures; for though these things may create some tickling in the senses (which seems to be a true notion of pleasure), yet they imagine that this does not arise from the thing itself, but from a depraved custom, which may so vitiate a man's taste that bitter things may pass for sweet, as women with child think pitch or tallow taste sweeter than honey; but as a man's sense, when corrupted either by a disease or some ill habit, does not change the nature of other things, so neither can it change the nature of pleasure.

They reckon up several sorts of pleasures, which they call true ones; some belong to the body, and others to the mind. The pleasures of the mind lie in knowledge, and in that delight which the contemplation of truth carries with it; to which they add the joyful reflections on a well-spent life, and the assured hopes of a future happiness. They divide the pleasures of the body into two sorts—the one is that which gives our senses some real delight, and is performed either by recruiting Nature and supplying those parts which feed the internal heat of life by eating and drinking, or when Nature is eased of any surcharge that oppresses it, when we are relieved from sudden pain, or that which arises from satisfying the appetite which Nature has wisely given to lead us to the propagation of the species. There is another kind of pleasure that arises neither from our receiving what the body requires, nor its being relieved when overcharged, and yet, by a secret unseen virtue, affects the senses, raises the passions, and strikes the mind with generous impressions—this is, the pleasure that arises from music. Another kind of bodily pleasure is that which results from an undisturbed and vigorous constitution of body, when life and active spirits seem to actuate every part. This lively health, when entirely free from all mixture of pain, of itself gives an inward pleasure, independent of all external objects of delight; and though this pleasure does not so powerfully affect us, nor act so strongly on the senses as some of the others, yet it may be esteemed as the greatest of all pleasures; and almost all the Utopians reckon it the foundation and basis of all the other joys of life, since this alone makes the state of life easy and desirable, and when this is wanting, a man is really capable of no other pleasure. They look upon freedom from pain, if it does not rise from perfect health, to be a state of stupidity rather than of pleasure. This subject has been very narrowly canvassed among them, and it has been debated whether a firm and entire health could be called a pleasure or not.

Some have thought that there was no pleasure but what was 'excited' by some sensible motion in the body. But this opinion has been long ago excluded from among them; so that now they almost universally agree that health is the greatest of all bodily pleasures; and that as there is a pain in sickness which is as opposite in its nature to pleasure as sickness itself is to health, so they hold that health is accompanied with pleasure. And if any should say that sickness is not really pain, but that it only carries pain along with it, they look upon that as a fetch of subtlety that does not much alter the matter. It is all one, in their opinion, whether it be said that health is in itself a pleasure, or that it begets a pleasure, as fire gives heat, so it be granted that all those whose health is entire have a true pleasure in the enjoyment of it.

And they reason thus:–'What is the pleasure of eating, but that a man's health, which had been weakened, does, with the assistance of food, drive away hunger, and so recruiting itself, recovers its former vigour? And being thus refreshed it finds a pleasure in that conflict; and if the conflict is pleasure, the victory must yet breed a greater pleasure, except we fancy that it becomes stupid as soon as it has obtained that which it pursued, and so neither knows nor rejoices in its own welfare.' If it is said that health cannot be felt, they absolutely deny it; for what man is in health, that does not perceive it when he is awake? Is there any man that is so dull and stupid as not to acknowledge that he feels a delight in health? And what is delight but another name for pleasure?

But, of all pleasures, they esteem those to be most valuable that lie in the mind, the chief of which arise out of true virtue and the witness of a good conscience. They account health the chief pleasure that belongs to the body; for they think that the pleasure of eating and drinking, and all the other delights of sense, are only so far desirable as they give or maintain health; but they are not pleasant in themselves otherwise than as they resist those impressions that our natural infirmities are still making upon us. For as a wise man desires rather to avoid diseases than to take physic, and to be freed from pain rather than to find ease by remedies, so it is more desirable not to need this sort of pleasure than to be obliged to indulge it.

If any man imagines that there is a real happiness in these enjoyments, he must then confess that he would be the happiest of all men if he were to lead his life in perpetual hunger, thirst, and itching, and, by consequence, in perpetual eating, drinking, and scratching himself; which any one may easily see would be not only a base, but a miserable, state of a life. These are, indeed, the lowest of pleasures, and the least pure, for we can never relish them but when they are mixed with the contrary pains. The pain of hunger must give us the pleasure of eating, and here the pain out-balances the pleasure. And as the pain is more vehement, so it lasts much longer; for as it begins before the pleasure, so it does not cease but with the pleasure that extinguishes it, and both expire together. They think, therefore, none of those pleasures are to be valued any further than as they are necessary; yet they rejoice in them, and with due gratitude acknowledge the tenderness of the great Author of Nature, who has planted in us appetites, by which those things that are necessary for our preservation are likewise made pleasant to us. For how miserable a thing would life be if those daily diseases of hunger and thirst were to be carried off by such bitter drugs as we must use for those diseases that return seldomer upon us! And thus these pleasant, as well as proper, gifts of Nature maintain the strength and the sprightliness of our bodies.

They also entertain themselves with the other delights let in at their eyes, their ears, and their nostrils as the pleasant relishes and seasoning of life, which Nature seems to have marked out peculiarly for man, since no other sort of animals contemplates the figure and beauty of the universe, nor is delighted with smells any further than as they distinguish meats by them; nor do they apprehend the concords or discords of sound. Yet, in all pleasures whatsoever, they take care that a lesser joy does not hinder a greater, and that pleasure may never breed pain, which they think always follows dishonest pleasures. But they think it madness for a man to wear out the beauty of his face or the force of his natural strength, to corrupt the sprightliness of his body by sloth and laziness, or to waste it by fasting; that it is madness to weaken the strength of his constitution and reject the other delights of life, unless by renouncing his own satisfaction he can either serve the public or promote the happiness of others, for which he expects a greater recompense from God. So that they look on such a course of life as the mark of a mind that is both cruel to itself and ungrateful to the Author of Nature, as if we would not be beholden to Him for His favours, and therefore rejects all His blessings; as one who should afflict himself for the empty shadow of virtue, or for no better end than to render himself capable of bearing those misfortunes which possibly will never happen.

This is their notion of virtue and of pleasure: they think that no man's reason can carry him to a truer idea of them unless some discovery from heaven should inspire him with sublimer notions. I have not now the leisure to examine whether they think right or wrong in this matter; nor do I judge it necessary, for I have only undertaken to give you an account of their constitution, but not to defend all their principles. I am sure that whatever may be said of their notions, there is not in the whole world either a better people or a happier government. Their bodies are vigorous and lively; and though they are but of a middle stature, and have neither the fruitfullest soil nor the purest air in the world; yet they fortify themselves so well, by their temperate course of life, against the unhealthiness of their air, and by their industry they so cultivate their soil, that there is nowhere to be seen a greater increase, both of corn and cattle, nor are there anywhere healthier men and freer from diseases; for one may there see reduced to practice not only all the art that the husbandman employs in manuring and improving an ill soil, but whole woods plucked up by the roots, and in other places new ones planted, where there were none before. Their principal motive for this is the convenience of carriage, that their timber may be either near their towns or growing on the banks of the sea, or of some rivers, so as to be floated to them; for it is a harder work to carry wood at any distance over land than corn. The people are industrious, apt to learn, as well as cheerful and pleasant, and none can endure more labour when it is necessary; but, except in that case, they love their ease.

OF THEIR LEARNING

They are unwearied pursuers of knowledge; for when we had given them some hints of the learning and discipline of the Greeks, concerning whom we only instructed them (for we know that there was nothing among the Romans, except their historians and their poets, that they would value much), it was strange to see how eagerly they were set on learning that language: we began to read a little of it to them, rather in compliance with their importunity than out of any hopes of their reaping from it any great advantage: but, after a very short trial, we found they made such progress, that we saw our labour was like to be more successful than we could have expected: they learned to write their characters and to pronounce their language so exactly, had so quick an apprehension, they remembered it so faithfully, and became so ready and correct in the use of it, that it would have looked like a miracle if the greater part of those whom we taught had not been men both of extraordinary capacity and of a fit age for instruction: they were, for the greatest part, chosen from among their learned men by their chief council, though some studied it of their own accord.

In three years' time they became masters of the whole language, so that they read the best of the Greek authors very exactly. I am, indeed, apt to think that they learned that language the more easily from its having some relation to their own. I believe that they were a colony of the Greeks; for though their language comes nearer the Persian, yet they retain many names, both for their towns and magistrates, that are of Greek derivation.

I happened to carry a great many books with me, instead of merchandise, when I sailed my fourth voyage; for I was so far from thinking of soon coming back, that I rather thought never to have returned at all, and I gave them all my books, among which were many of Plato's and some of Aristotle's works: I had also Theophrastus on Plants, which, to my great regret, was imperfect; for having laid it carelessly by, while we were at sea, a monkey had seized upon it, and in many places torn out the leaves. They have no books of grammar but Lascares, for I did not carry Theodorus with me; nor have they any dictionaries but Hesichius and Dioscerides. They esteem Plutarch highly, and were much taken with Lucian's wit and with his pleasant way of writing. As for the poets, they have Aristophanes, Homer, Euripides, and Sophocles of Aldus's edition; and for historians, Thucydides, Herodotus, and Herodian.

One of my companions, Thricius Apinatus, happened to carry with him some of Hippocrates's works and Galen's Microtechne, which they hold in great estimation; for though there is no nation in the world that needs physic so little as they do, yet there is not any that honours it so much; they reckon the knowledge of it one of the pleasantest and most profitable parts of philosophy, by which, as they search into the secrets of nature, so they not only find this study highly agreeable, but think that such inquiries are very acceptable to the Author of nature; and imagine, that as He, like the inventors of curious engines amongst mankind, has exposed this great machine of the universe to the view of the only creatures capable of contemplating it, so an exact and curious observer, who admires His workmanship, is much more acceptable to Him than one of the herd, who, like a beast incapable of reason, looks on this glorious scene with the eyes of a dull and unconcerned spectator.

The minds of the Utopians, when fenced with a love for learning, are very ingenious in discovering all such arts as are necessary to carry it to perfection. Two things they owe to us, the manufacture of paper and the art of printing; yet they are not so entirely indebted to us for these discoveries but that a great part of the invention was their own. We showed them some books printed by Aldus, we explained to them the way of making paper and the mystery of printing; but, as we had never practised these arts, we described them in a crude and superficial manner. They seized the hints we gave them; and though at first they could not arrive at perfection, yet by making many essays they at last found out and corrected all their errors and conquered every difficulty. Before this they only wrote on parchment, on reeds, or on the barks of trees; but now they have established the manufactures of paper and set up printing presses, so that, if they had but a good number of Greek authors, they would be quickly supplied with many copies of them: at present, though they have no more than those I have mentioned, yet, by several impressions, they have multiplied them into many thousands.

If any man was to go among them that had some extraordinary talent, or that by much travelling had observed the customs of many nations (which made us to be so well received), he would receive a hearty welcome, for they are very desirous to know the state of the whole world. Very few go among them on the account of traffic; for what can a man carry to them but iron, or gold, or silver? which merchants desire rather to export than import to a strange country:

and as for their exportation, they think it better to manage that themselves than to leave it to foreigners, for by this means, as they understand the state of the neighbouring countries better, so they keep up the art of navigation which cannot be maintained but by much practice.

OF THEIR SLAVES

They do not make slaves of prisoners of war, except those that are taken in battle, nor of the sons of their slaves, nor of those of other nations: the slaves among them are only such as are condemned to that state of life for the commission of some crime, or, which is more common, such as their merchants find condemned to die in those parts to which they trade, whom they sometimes redeem at low rates, and in other places have them for nothing. They are kept at perpetual labour, and are always chained, but with this difference, that their own natives are treated much worse than others: they are considered as more profligate than the rest, and since they could not be restrained by the advantages of so excellent an education, are judged worthy of harder usage. Another sort of slaves are the poor of the neighbouring countries, who offer of their own accord to come and serve them: they treat these better, and use them in all other respects as well as their own countrymen, except their imposing more labour upon them, which is no hard task to those that have been accustomed to it; and if any of these have a mind to go back to their own country, which, indeed, falls out but seldom, as they do not force them to stay, so they do not send them away empty-handed.

OF THEIR DEATHS

I have already told you with what care they look after their sick, so that nothing is left undone that can contribute either to their case or health; and for those who are taken with fixed and incurable diseases, they use all possible ways to cherish them and to make their lives as comfortable as possible. They visit them often and take great pains to make their time pass off easily; but when any is taken with a torturing and lingering pain, so that there is no hope either of recovery or ease, the priests and magistrates come and exhort them, that, since they are now unable to go on with the business of life, are become a burden to themselves and to all about them, and they have really out-lived themselves, they should no longer nourish such a rooted distemper, but choose rather to die since they cannot live but in much misery; being assured that if they thus deliver themselves from torture, or are willing that others should do it, they shall be happy after death: since, by their acting thus, they lose none of the pleasures, but only the troubles of life, they think they behave not only reasonably but in a manner consistent with religion and piety; because they follow the advice given them by their priests, who are the expounders of the will of God.

Such as are wrought on by these persuasions either starve themselves of their own accord, or take opium, and by that means die without pain. But no man is forced on this way of ending his life; and if they cannot be persuaded to it, this does not induce them to fail in their attendance and care of them: but as they believe that a voluntary death, when it is chosen upon such an authority, is very honourable, so if any man takes away his own life without the approbation of the priests and the senate, they give him none of the honours of a decent funeral, but throw his body into a ditch.

OF THEIR MARRIAGES

Their women are not married before eighteen nor their men before two-and-twenty, and if any of them run into forbidden embraces before marriage they are severely punished, and the privilege of marriage is denied them unless they can obtain a special warrant from the Prince. Such disorders cast a great reproach upon the master and mistress of the family in which they happen, for it is supposed that they have failed in their duty. The reason of punishing this so severely is, because they think that if they were not strictly restrained from all vagrant appetites, very few would engage in a state in which they venture the quiet of their whole lives, by being confined to one person, and are obliged to endure all the inconveniences with which it is accompanied.

In choosing their wives they use a method that would appear to us very absurd and ridiculous, but it is constantly observed among them, and is accounted perfectly consistent with wisdom. Before marriage some grave matron presents the bride, naked, whether she is a virgin or a widow, to the bridegroom, and after that some grave man presents the bridegroom, naked, to the bride. We, indeed, both laughed at this, and condemned it as very indecent. But they, on the other hand, wondered at the folly of the men of all other nations, who, if they are but to buy a horse of a small value, are so cautious that they will see every part of him, and take off both his saddle and all his other tackle, that there may be no secret ulcer hid under any of them, and that yet in the choice of a wife, on which depends the happiness or unhappiness of the rest of his life, a man should venture upon trust, and only see about a handsbreadth of the face, all the rest of the body being covered, under which may lie hid what may be contagious as well as loathsome. All men are not so wise as to choose a woman only for her good qualities, and even wise men consider the body as that which adds not a little to the mind, and it is certain there may be some such deformity covered with clothes as may totally alienate a man from his wife, when it is too late to part with her; if such a thing is discovered after marriage a man has no remedy but patience; they, therefore, think it is reasonable that there should be good provision made against such mischievous frauds.

There was so much the more reason for them to make a regulation in this matter, because they are the only people of those parts that neither allow of polygamy nor of divorces, except in the case of adultery or insufferable perverseness, for in these cases the Senate dissolves the marriage and grants the injured person leave to marry again; but the guilty are made infamous and are never allowed the privilege of a second marriage. None are suffered to put away their wives against their wills, from any great calamity that may have fallen on their persons, for they look on it as the height of cruelty and treachery to abandon either of the married persons when they need most the tender care of their consort, and that chiefly in the case of old age, which, as it carries many diseases along with it, so it is a disease of itself.

But it frequently falls out that when a married couple do not well agree, they, by mutual consent, separate, and find out other persons with whom they hope they may live more happily; yet this is not done without obtaining leave of the Senate, which never admits of a divorce but upon a strict inquiry made, both by the senators and their wives, into the grounds upon which it is desired, and even when they are satisfied concerning the reasons of it they go on but slowly, for they imagine that too great easiness in granting leave for new marriages would very much shake the kindness of married people.

They punish severely those that defile the marriage bed; if both parties are married they are divorced, and the injured persons may marry one another, or whom they please, but the adulterer and the adulteress are condemned to slavery, yet if either of the injured persons cannot shake off the love of the married person they may live with them still in that state, but they must follow them to that labour to which the slaves are condemned, and sometimes the repentance of the condemned, together with the unshaken kindness of the innocent and injured person, has prevailed so far with the Prince that he has taken off the sentence; but those that relapse after they are once pardoned are punished with death.

OF THEIR LAWS AND PUNISHMENTS

Their law does not determine the punishment for other crimes, but that is left to the Senate, to temper it according to the circumstances of the fact. Husbands have power to correct their wives and parents to chastise their children, unless the fault is so great that a public punishment is thought necessary for striking terror into others. For the most part slavery is the punishment even of the greatest crimes, for as that is no less terrible to the criminals themselves than death, so they think the preserving them in a state of servitude is more for the interest of the commonwealth than killing them, since, as their labour is a greater benefit to the public than their death could be, so the sight of their misery is a more lasting terror to other men than that which would be given by their death.

If their slaves rebel, and will not bear their yoke and submit to the labour that is enjoined them, they are treated as wild beasts that cannot be kept in order, neither by a prison nor by their chains, and are at last put to death. But those who bear their punishment patiently, and are so much wrought on by that pressure that lies so hard on them, that it appears they are really more troubled for the crimes they have committed than for the miseries they suffer, are not out of hope, but that, at last, either the Prince will, by his prerogative, or the people, by their intercession, restore them again to their liberty, or, at least, very much mitigate their slavery.

He that tempts a married woman to adultery is no less severely punished than he that commits it, for they believe that a deliberate design to commit a crime is equal to the fact itself, since its not taking effect does not make the person that miscarried in his attempt at all the less guilty.

They take great pleasure in fools, and as it is thought a base and unbecoming thing to use them ill, so they do not think it amiss for people to divert themselves with their folly; and, in their opinion, this is a great advantage to the fools themselves; for if men were so sullen and severe as not at all to please themselves with their ridiculous behaviour and foolish sayings, which is all that they can do to recommend themselves to others, it could not be expected that they would be so well provided for nor so tenderly used as they must otherwise be.

If any man should reproach another for his being misshaped or imperfect in any part of his body, it would not at all be thought a reflection on the person so treated, but it would be accounted scandalous in him that had upbraided another with what he could not help. It is thought a sign of a sluggish and sordid mind not to preserve carefully one's natural beauty; but it is likewise infamous among them to use paint. They all see that no beauty recommends a wife so much to her husband as the probity of her life and her obedience; for as some few are caught and held only by beauty, so all are attracted by the other excellences which charm all the world.

As they fright men from committing crimes by punishments, so they invite them to the love of virtue by public honours; therefore they erect statues to the memories of such worthy men as have deserved well of their country, and set these in their market-places, both to perpetuate the remembrance of their actions and to be an incitement to their posterity to follow their example.

If any man aspires to any office he is sure never to compass it. They all live easily together, for none of the magistrates are either insolent or cruel to the people; they affect rather to be called fathers, and, by being really so, they well deserve the name; and the people pay them all the marks of honour the more freely because none are exacted from them. The Prince himself has no distinction, either of garments or of a crown; but is only distinguished by a sheaf of corn carried before him; as the High Priest is also known by his being preceded by a person carrying a wax light.

They have but few laws, and such is their constitution that they need not many. They very much condemn other nations whose laws, together with the commentaries on them, swell up to so many volumes; for they think it an unreasonable thing to oblige men to obey a body of laws that are both of such a bulk, and so dark as not to be read and understood by every one of the subjects.

They have no lawyers among them, for they consider them as a sort of people whose profession it is to disguise matters and to wrest the laws, and, therefore, they think it is much better that every man should plead his own cause, and trust it to the judge, as in other places the client trusts it to a counsellor; by this means they both cut off many delays and find out truth more certainly; for after the parties have laid open the merits of the cause, without those artifices which lawyers are apt to suggest, the judge examines the whole matter, and supports the simplicity of such well-meaning persons, whom otherwise crafty men would be sure to run down; and thus they avoid those evils which appear very remarkably among all those nations that labour under a vast load of laws.

Every one of them is skilled in their law; for, as it is a very short study, so the plainest meaning of which words are capable is always the sense of their laws; and they argue thus: all laws are promulgated for this end, that every man may know his duty; and, therefore, the plainest and most obvious sense of the words is that which ought to be put upon them, since a more refined exposition cannot be easily comprehended, and would only serve to make the laws become useless to the greater part of mankind, and especially to those who need most the direction of them; for it is all one not to make a law at all or to couch it in such terms that, without a quick apprehension and much study, a man cannot find out the true meaning of it, since the generality of mankind are both so dull, and so much employed in their several trades, that they have neither the leisure nor the capacity requisite for such an inquiry.

OF THEIR FOREIGN POLICIES

Some of their neighbours, who are masters of their own liberties (having long ago, by the assistance of the Utopians, shaken off the yoke of tyranny, and being much taken with those virtues which they observe among them), have come to desire that they would send magistrates to govern them, some changing them every year, and others every five years; at the end of their government they bring them back to Utopia, with great expressions of honour and esteem, and carry away others to govern in their stead. In this they seem to have fallen upon a very good expedient for their own happiness and safety; for since the good or ill condition of a nation depends so much upon their magistrates, they could not have made a better choice than by pitching on men whom no advantages can bias; for wealth is of no use to them, since they must so soon go back to their own country, and they, being strangers among them, are not engaged in any of their heats or animosities; and it is certain that when public judicatories are swayed, either by avarice or partial affections, there must follow a dissolution of justice, the chief sinew of society.

The Utopians call those nations that come and ask magistrates from them Neighbours; but those to whom they have been of more particular service, Friends; and as all other nations are perpetually either making leagues or breaking them, they never enter into an alliance with any state. They think leagues are useless things, and believe that if the common ties of humanity do not knit men together, the faith of promises will have no great effect; and they are the more confirmed in this by what they see among the nations round about them, who are no strict observers of leagues and treaties.

We know how religiously they are observed in Europe, more particularly where the Christian doctrine is received, among whom they are sacred and inviolable! Which is partly owing to the justice and goodness of the princes themselves, and partly to the reverence they pay to the popes, who, as they are the most religious observers of their own promises, so they exhort all other princes to perform theirs, and, when fainter methods do not prevail, they compel them to it by the severity of the pastoral censure, and think that it would be the most indecent thing possible if men who are particularly distinguished by the title of 'The Faithful' should not religiously keep the faith of their treaties.

But in that new-found world, which is not more distant from us in situation than the people are in their manners and course of life, there is no trusting to leagues, even though they were made with all the pomp of the most sacred ceremonies; on the contrary, they are on this account the sooner broken, some slight pretence being found in the words of the treaties, which are purposely couched in such ambiguous terms that they can never be so strictly bound but they will always find some loophole to escape at, and thus they break both their leagues and their faith; and this is done with such impudence, that those very men who value themselves on having suggested these expedients to their princes would, with a haughty scorn, declaim against such craft; or, to speak plainer, such fraud and deceit, if they found private men make use of it in their bargains, and would readily say that they deserved to be hanged.

By this means it is that all sort of justice passes in the world for a low-spirited and vulgar virtue, far below the dignity of royal greatness–or at least there are set up two sorts of justice; the one is mean and creeps on the ground, and, therefore, becomes none but the lower part of mankind, and so must be kept in severely by many restraints, that it may not break out beyond the bounds that are set to it; the other is the peculiar virtue of princes, which, as it is more majestic than that which becomes the rabble, so takes a freer compass, and thus lawful and unlawful are only measured by pleasure and interest. These practices of the princes that lie about Utopia, who make so little account of their faith, seem to be the reasons that determine them to engage in no confederacy. Perhaps they would change their mind if they lived among us; but yet, though treaties were more religiously observed, they would still dislike the custom of making them, since the world has taken up a false maxim upon it, as if there were no tie of nature uniting one nation to another, only separated perhaps by a mountain or a river, and that all were born in a state of hostility, and so might lawfully do all that mischief to their neighbours against which there is no provision made by treaties; and that when treaties are made they do not cut off the enmity or restrain the licence of preying upon each other, if, by the unskilfulness of wording them, there are not effectual provisos made against them; they, on the other hand, judge that no man is to be esteemed our enemy that has never injured us, and that the partnership of human nature is instead of a league; and that kindness and good nature unite men more effectually and with greater strength than any agreements whatsoever, since thereby the engagements of men's hearts become stronger than the bond and obligation of words.

OF THEIR MILITARY DISCIPLINE

They detest war as a very brutal thing, and which, to the reproach of human nature, is more practised by men than by any sort of beasts. They, in opposition to the sentiments of almost all other nations, think that there is nothing more inglorious than that glory that is gained by war; and therefore, though they accustom themselves daily to military exercises and the discipline of war, in which not only their men, but their women likewise, are trained up, that, in cases of necessity, they may not be quite useless, yet they do not rashly engage in war, unless it be either to defend themselves or their friends from any unjust aggressors, or, out of good nature or in compassion, assist an oppressed nation in shaking off the yoke of tyranny. They, indeed, help their friends not only in defensive but also in offensive wars; but they never do that unless they had been consulted before the breach was made, and, being satisfied with the grounds on which they went, they had found that all demands of reparation were rejected, so that a war was unavoidable.

This they think to be not only just when one neighbour makes an inroad on another by public order, and carries away the spoils, but when the merchants of one country are oppressed in another, either under pretence of some unjust laws, or by the perverse wresting of good ones. This they count a juster cause of war than the other, because those injuries are done under some colour of laws. This was the only ground of that war in which they engaged with the Nephelogetes against the Aleopolitanes, a little before our time; for the merchants of the former having, as they thought, met with great injustice among the latter, which (whether it was in itself right or wrong) drew on a terrible war, in which many of their neighbours were engaged; and their keenness in carrying it on being supported by their strength in maintaining it, it not only shook some very flourishing states and very much afflicted others, but, after a series of much mischief ended in the entire conquest and slavery of the Aleopolitanes, who, though before the war they were in all respects much superior to the Nephelogetes, were yet subdued; but, though the Utopians had assisted them in the war, yet they pretended to no share of the spoil.

But, though they so vigorously assist their friends in obtaining reparation for the injuries they have received in affairs of this nature, yet, if any such frauds were committed against themselves, provided no violence was done to their persons, they would only, on their being refused satisfaction, forbear trading with such a people. This is not because they consider their neighbours more than their own citizens; but, since their neighbours trade every one upon his own stock, fraud is a more sensible injury to them than it is to the Utopians, among whom the public, in such a case, only suffers, as they expect no thing in return for the merchandise they export but that in which they so much abound, and is of little use to them, the loss does not much affect them. They think, therefore, it would be too severe to revenge a loss attended with so little inconvenience, either to their lives or their subsistence, with the death of many persons; but if any of their people are either killed or wounded wrongfully, whether it be done by public authority, or only by private men, as soon as they hear of it they send ambassadors, and demand that the guilty persons may be delivered up to them, and if that is denied, they declare war; but if it be complied with, the offenders are condemned either to death or slavery.

They would be both troubled and ashamed of a bloody victory over their enemies; and think it would be as foolish a purchase as to buy the most valuable goods at too high a rate. And in no victory do they glory so much as in that which is gained by dexterity and good conduct without bloodshed. In such cases they appoint public triumphs, and erect trophies to the honour of those who have succeeded; for then do they reckon that a man acts suitably to his nature, when he conquers his enemy in such a way as that no other creature but a man could be capable of, and that is by the strength of his understanding. Bears, lions, boars, wolves, and dogs, and all other animals, employ their bodily force one against another, in which, as many of them are superior to men, both in strength and fierceness, so they are all subdued by his reason and understanding.

The only design of the Utopians in war is to obtain that by force which, if it had been granted them in time, would have prevented the war; or, if that cannot be done, to take so severe a revenge on those that have injured them that they may be terrified from doing the like for the time to come. By these ends they measure all their designs, and manage them so, that it is visible that the appetite of fame or vainglory does not work so much on there as a just care of their own security.

As soon as they declare war, they take care to have a great many schedules, that are sealed with their common seal, affixed in the most conspicuous places of their enemies' country. This is carried secretly, and done in many places all at once. In these they promise great rewards to such as shall kill the prince, and lesser in proportion to such as shall kill any other persons who are those on whom, next to the prince himself, they cast the chief balance of the war. And they double the sum to him that, instead of killing the person so marked out, shall take him alive, and put him in their hands. They offer not only indemnity, but rewards, to such of the persons themselves that are so marked, if they will act against their countrymen. By this means those that are named in their schedules become not only distrustful of their fellow-citizens, but are jealous of one another, and are much distracted by fear and danger; for it has often fallen out that many of them, and even the prince himself, have been betrayed, by those in whom they have trusted most; for the rewards that the Utopians offer are so immeasurably great, that there is no sort of crime to which men cannot be drawn by them. They consider the risk that those run who undertake such services, and offer a recompense proportioned to the danger–not only a vast deal of gold, but great revenues in lands, that lie among other nations that are their friends, where they may go and enjoy them very securely; and they observe the promises they make of their kind most religiously.

They very much approve of this way of corrupting their enemies, though it appears to others to be base and cruel; but they look on it as a wise course, to make an end of what would be otherwise a long war, without so much as hazarding one battle to decide it. They think it likewise an act of mercy and love to mankind to prevent the great slaughter of those that must otherwise be killed in the progress of the war, both on their own side and on that of their enemies, by the death of a few that are most guilty; and that in so doing they are kind even to their enemies, and pity them no less than their own people, as knowing that the greater part of them do not engage in the war of their own accord, but are driven into it by the passions of their prince.

If this method does not succeed with them, then they sow seeds of contention among their enemies, and animate the prince's brother, or some of the nobility, to aspire to the crown. If they cannot disunite them by domestic broils, then they engage their neighbours against them, and make them set on foot some old pretensions, which are never wanting to princes when they have occasion for them. These they plentifully supply with money, though but very sparingly with any auxiliary troops; for they are so tender of their own people that they would not willingly exchange one of them, even with the prince of their enemies' country.

But as they keep their gold and silver only for such an occasion, so, when that offers itself, they easily part with it; since it would be no convenience to them, though they should reserve nothing of it to themselves. For besides the wealth that they have among them at home, they have a vast treasure abroad; many nations round about them being deep in their debt: so that they hire soldiers from all places for carrying on their wars; but chiefly from the Zapolets, who live five hundred miles east of Utopia. They are a rude, wild, and fierce nation, who delight in the woods and rocks, among which they were born and bred up. They are hardened both against heat, cold, and labour, and know nothing of the delicacies of life. They do not apply themselves to agriculture, nor do they care either for their houses or their clothes: cattle is all that they look after; and for the greatest part they live either by hunting or upon rapine; and are made, as it were, only for war.

They watch all opportunities of engaging in it, and very readily embrace such as are offered them. Great numbers of them will frequently go out, and offer themselves for a very low pay, to serve any that will employ them: they know none of the arts of life, but those that lead to the taking it away; they serve those that hire them, both with much courage and great fidelity; but will not engage to serve for any determined time, and agree upon such terms, that the next day they may go over to the enemies of those whom they serve if they offer them a greater encouragement; and will, perhaps, return to them the day after that upon a higher advance of their pay. There are few wars in which they make not a considerable part of the armies of both sides: so it often falls out that they who are related, and were hired in the same country, and so have lived long and familiarly together, forgetting both their relations and former friendship, kill one another upon no other consideration than that of being hired to it for a little money by princes of different interests; and such a regard have they for money that they are easily wrought on by the difference of one penny a day to change sides. So entirely does their avarice influence them; and yet this money, which they value so highly, is of little use to them; for what they purchase thus with their blood they quickly waste on luxury, which among them is but of a poor and miserable form.

This nation serves the Utopians against all people whatsoever, for they pay higher than any other. The Utopians hold this for a maxim, that as they seek out the best sort of men for their own use at home, so they make use of this worst sort of men for the consumption of war; and therefore they hire them with the offers of vast rewards to expose themselves to all sorts of hazards, out of which the greater part never returns to claim their promises; yet they make them good most religiously to such as escape. This animates them to adventure again, whenever there is occasion for it; for the Utopians are not at all troubled how many of these happen to be killed, and reckon it a service done to mankind if they could be a means to deliver the world from such a lewd and vicious sort of people, that seem to have run together, as to the drain of human nature.

Next to these, they are served in their wars with those upon whose account they undertake them, and with the auxiliary troops of their other friends, to whom they join a few of their own people, and send some man of eminent and approved virtue to command in chief. There are two sent with him, who, during his command, are but private men, but the first is to succeed him if he should happen to be either killed or taken; and, in case of the like misfortune to him, the third comes in his place; and thus they provide against all events, that such accidents as may befall their generals may not endanger their armies.

When they draw out troops of their own people, they take such out of every city as freely offer themselves, for none are forced to go against their wills, since they think that if any man is pressed that wants courage, he will not only act faintly, but by his cowardice dishearten others. But if an invasion is made on their country, they make use of such men, if they have good bodies, though they are not brave; and either put them aboard their ships, or place them on the walls of their towns, that being so posted, they may find no opportunity of flying away; and thus either shame, the heat of action, or the impossibility of flying, bears down their cowardice; they often make a virtue of necessity, and behave themselves well, because nothing else is left them.

But as they force no man to go into any foreign war against his will, so they do not hinder those women who are willing to go along with their husbands; on the contrary, they encourage and praise them, and they stand often next their husbands in the front of the army. They also place together those who are related, parents, and children, kindred, and those that are mutually allied, near one another; that those whom nature has inspired with the greatest zeal for assisting one another may be the nearest and readiest to do it; and it is matter of great reproach if husband or wife survive one another, or if a child survives his parent, and therefore when they come to be engaged in action, they continue to fight to the last man, if their enemies stand before them: and as they use all prudent methods to avoid the endangering their own men, and if it is possible let all the action and danger fall upon the troops that they hire, so if it becomes necessary for themselves to engage, they then charge with as much courage as they avoided it before with prudence: nor is it a fierce charge at first, but it increases by degrees; and as they continue in action, they grow more obstinate, and press harder upon the enemy, insomuch that they will much sooner die than give ground; for the certainty that their children will be well looked after when they are dead frees them from all that anxiety concerning them which often masters men of great courage; and thus they are animated by a noble and invincible resolution.

Their skill in military affairs increases their courage: and the wise sentiments which, according to the laws of their country, are instilled into them in their education, give additional vigour to their minds: for as they do not undervalue life so as prodigally to throw it away, they are not so indecently fond of it as to preserve it by base and unbecoming methods. In the greatest heat of action the bravest of their youth, who have devoted themselves to that service, single out the general of their enemies, set on him either openly or by ambuscade; pursue him everywhere, and when spent and wearied out, are relieved by others, who never give over the pursuit, either attacking him with close weapons when they can get near him, or with those which wound at a distance, when others get in between them. So that, unless he secures himself by flight, they seldom fail at last to kill or to take him prisoner.

When they have obtained a victory, they kill as few as possible, and are much more bent on taking many prisoners than on killing those that fly before them. Nor do they ever let their men so loose in the pursuit of their enemies as not to retain an entire body still in order; so that if they have been forced to engage the last of their battalions before they could gain the day, they will rather let their enemies all escape than pursue them when their own army is in disorder; remembering well what has often fallen out to themselves, that when the main body of their army has been quite defeated and broken, when their enemies, imagining the victory obtained, have let themselves loose into an irregular pursuit, a few of them that lay for a reserve, waiting a fit opportunity, have fallen on them in their chase, and when straggling in disorder, and apprehensive of no danger, but counting the day their own, have turned the whole action, and, wresting out of their hands a victory that seemed certain and undoubted, while the vanquished have suddenly become victorious.

It is hard to tell whether they are more dexterous in laying or avoiding ambushes. They sometimes seem to fly when it is far from their thoughts; and when they intend to give ground, they do it so that it is very hard to find out their design. If they see they are ill posted, or are like to be overpowered by numbers, they then either march off in the night with great silence, or by some stratagem delude their enemies. If they retire in the day-time, they do it in such order that it is no less dangerous to fall upon them in a retreat than in a march. They fortify their camps with a deep and large trench; and throw up the earth that is dug out of it for a wall; nor do they employ only their slaves in this, but the whole army works at it, except those that are then upon the guard; so that when so many hands are at work, a great line and a strong fortification is finished in so short a time that it is scarce credible.

Their armour is very strong for defence, and yet is not so heavy as to make them uneasy in their marches; they can even swim with it. All that are trained up to war practise swimming. Both horse and foot make great use of arrows, and are very expert. They have no swords, but fight with a pole-axe that is both sharp and heavy, by which they thrust or strike down an enemy. They are very good at finding out warlike machines, and disguise them so well that the enemy does not perceive them till he feels the use of them; so that he cannot prepare such a defence as would render them useless; the chief consideration had in the making them is that they may be easily carried and managed.

If they agree to a truce, they observe it so religiously that no provocations will make them break it. They never lay their enemies' country waste nor burn their corn, and even in their marches they take all possible care that neither horse nor foot may tread it down, for they do not know but that they may have use for it themselves. They hurt no man whom they find disarmed, unless he is a spy. When a town is surrendered to them, they take it into their protection; and when they carry a place by storm they never plunder it, but put those only to the sword that oppose the rendering of it up, and make the rest of the garrison slaves, but for the other inhabitants, they do them no hurt; and if any of them had advised a surrender, they give them good rewards out of the estates of those that they condemn, and distribute the rest among their auxiliary troops, but they themselves take no share of the spoil.

When a war is ended, they do not oblige their friends to reimburse their expenses; but they obtain them of the conquered, either in money, which they keep for the next occasion, or in lands, out of which a constant revenue is to be paid them; by many increases the revenue which they draw out from several countries on such occasions is now risen to above 700,000 ducats a year. They send some of their own people to receive these revenues, who have orders to live magnificently and like princes, by which means they consume much of it upon the place; and either bring over the rest to Utopia or lend it to that nation in which it lies. This they most commonly do, unless some great occasion, which falls out but very seldom, should oblige them to call for it all. It is out of these lands that they assign rewards to such as they encourage to adventure on desperate attempts. If any prince that engages in war with them is making preparations for invading their country, they prevent him, and make his country the seat of the war; for they do not willingly suffer any war to break in upon their island; and if that should happen, they would only defend themselves by their own people; but would not call for auxiliary troops to their assistance.

OF THE RELIGIONS OF THE UTOPIANS

There are several sorts of religions, not only in different parts of the island, but even in every town; some worshipping the sun, others the moon or one of the planets. Some worship such men as have been eminent in former times for virtue or glory, not only as ordinary deities, but as the supreme god. Yet the greater and wiser sort of them worship none of these, but adore one eternal, invisible, infinite, and incomprehensible Deity; as a Being that is far above all our apprehensions, that is spread over the whole universe, not by His bulk, but by His power and virtue; Him they call the Father of All, and acknowledge that the beginnings, the increase, the progress, the vicissitudes, and the end of all things come only from Him; nor do they offer divine honours to any but to Him alone. And, indeed, though they differ concerning other things, yet all agree in this: that they think there is one Supreme Being that made and governs the world, whom they call, in the language of their country, Mithras. They differ in this: that one thinks the god whom he worships is this Supreme Being, and another thinks that his idol is that god; but they all agree in one principle, that whoever is this Supreme Being, He is also that great essence to whose glory and majesty all honours are ascribed by the consent of all nations.

By degrees they fall off from the various superstitions that are among them, and grow up to that one religion that is the best and most in request; and there is no doubt to be made, but that all the others had vanished long ago, if some of those who advised them to lay aside their superstitions had not met with some unhappy accidents, which, being considered as inflicted by heaven, made them afraid that the god whose worship had like to have been abandoned had interposed and revenged themselves on those who despised their authority.

After they had heard from us an account of the doctrine, the course of life, and the miracles of Christ, and of the wonderful constancy of so many martyrs, whose blood, so willingly offered up by them, was the chief occasion of spreading their religion over a vast number of nations, it is not to be imagined how inclined they were to receive it. I shall not determine whether this proceeded from any secret inspiration of God, or whether it was because it seemed so favourable to that community of goods, which is an opinion so particular as well as so dear to them; since they perceived that Christ and His followers lived by that rule, and that it was still kept up in some communities among the sincerest sort of Christians. From whichsoever of these motives it might be, true it is, that many of them came over to our religion, and were initiated into it by baptism. But as two of our number were dead, so none of the four that survived were in priests' orders, we, therefore, could only baptise them, so that, to our great regret, they could not partake of the other sacraments, that can only be administered by priests, but they are instructed concerning them and long most vehemently for them. They have had great disputes among themselves, whether one chosen by them to be a priest would not be thereby qualified to do all the things that belong to that character, even though he had no authority derived from the Pope, and they seemed to be resolved to choose some for that employment, but they had not done it when I left them.

Those among them that have not received our religion do not fright any from it, and use none ill that goes over to it, so that all the while I was there one man was only punished on this occasion. He being newly baptised did, notwithstanding all that we could say to the contrary, dispute publicly concerning the Christian religion, with more zeal than discretion, and with so much heat, that he not only preferred our worship to theirs, but condemned all their rites as profane, and cried out against all that adhered to them as impious and sacrilegious persons, that were to be damned to everlasting burnings. Upon his having frequently preached in this manner he was seized, and after trial he was condemned to banishment, not for having disparaged their religion, but for his inflaming the people to sedition; for this is one of their most ancient laws, that no man ought to be punished for his religion.

At the first constitution of their government, Utopus having understood that before his coming among them the old inhabitants had been engaged in great quarrels concerning religion, by which they were so divided among themselves, that he found it an easy thing to conquer them, since, instead of uniting their forces against him, every different party in religion fought by themselves. After he had subdued them he made a law that every man might be of what religion he pleased, and might endeavour to draw others to it by the force of argument and by amicable and modest ways, but without bitterness against those of other opinions; but that he ought to use no other force but that of persuasion, and was neither to mix with it reproaches nor violence; and such as did otherwise were to be condemned to banishment or slavery.

This law was made by Utopus, not only for preserving the public peace, which he saw suffered much by daily contentions and irreconcilable heats, but because he thought the interest of religion itself required it. He judged it not fit to determine anything rashly; and seemed to doubt whether those different forms of religion might not all come from God, who might inspire man in a different manner, and be pleased with this variety; he therefore thought it indecent and foolish for any man to threaten and terrify another to make him believe what did not appear to him to be true. And supposing that only one religion was really true, and the rest false, he imagined that the native force of truth would at last break forth and shine bright, if supported only by the strength of argument, and attended to with a gentle and unprejudiced mind; while, on the other hand, if such debates were carried on with violence and tumults, as the most wicked are always the most obstinate, so the best and most holy religion might be choked with superstition, as corn is with briars and thorns; he therefore left men wholly to their liberty, that they might be free to believe as they should see cause; only he made a solemn and severe law against such as should so far degenerate from the dignity of human nature, as to think that our souls died with our bodies, or that the world was governed by chance, without a wise overruling Providence: for they all formerly believed that there was a state of rewards and punishments to the good and bad after this life; and they now look on those that think otherwise as scarce fit to be counted men, since they degrade so noble a being as the soul, and reckon it no better than a beast's: thus they are far from looking on such men as fit for human society, or to be citizens of a well-ordered commonwealth; since a man of such principles must needs, as oft as he dares do it, despise all their laws and customs: for there is no doubt to be made, that a man who is afraid of nothing but the law, and apprehends nothing after death, will not scruple to break through all the laws of his country, either by fraud or force, when by this means he may satisfy his appetites.

They never raise any that hold these maxims, either to honours or offices, nor employ them in any public trust, but despise them, as men of base and sordid minds. Yet they do not punish them, because they lay this down as a maxim, that a man cannot make himself believe anything he pleases; nor do they drive any to dissemble their thoughts by threatenings, so that men are not tempted to lie or disguise their opinions; which being a sort of fraud, is abhorred by the Utopians: they take care indeed to prevent their disputing in defence of these opinions, especially before the common people: but they suffer, and even encourage them to dispute concerning them in private with their priest, and other grave men, being confident that they will be cured of those mad opinions by having reason laid before them. There are many among them that run far to the other extreme, though it is neither thought an ill nor unreasonable opinion, and therefore is not at all discouraged. They think that the souls of beasts are immortal, though far inferior to the dignity of the human soul, and not capable of so great a happiness.

They are almost all of them very firmly persuaded that good men will be infinitely happy in another state: so that though they are compassionate to all that are sick, yet they lament no man's death, except they see him loath to part with life; for they look on this as a very ill presage, as if the soul, conscious to itself of guilt, and quite hopeless, was afraid to leave the body, from some secret hints of approaching misery. They think that such a man's appearance before God cannot be acceptable to Him, who being called on, does not go out cheerfully, but is backward and unwilling, and is as it were dragged to it. They are struck with horror when they see any die in this manner, and carry them out in silence and with sorrow, and praying God that He would be merciful to the errors of the departed soul, they lay the body in the ground: but when any die cheerfully, and full of hope, they do not mourn for them, but sing hymns when they carry out their bodies, and commending their souls very earnestly to God: their whole behaviour is then rather grave than sad, they burn the body, and set up a pillar where the pile was made, with an inscription to the honour of the deceased. When they come from the funeral, they discourse of his good life, and worthy actions, but speak of nothing oftener and with more pleasure than of his serenity at the hour of death.

They think such respect paid to the memory of good men is both the greatest incitement to engage others to follow their example, and the most acceptable worship that can be offered them; for they believe that though by the imperfection of human sight they are invisible to us, yet they are present among us, and hear those discourses that pass concerning themselves. They believe it inconsistent with the happiness of departed souls not to be at liberty to be where they will: and do not imagine them capable of the ingratitude of not desiring to see those friends with whom they lived on earth in the strictest bonds of love and kindness: besides, they are persuaded that good men, after death, have these affections; and all other good dispositions increased rather than diminished, and therefore conclude that they are still among the living, and observe all they say or do. From hence they engage in all their affairs with the greater confidence of success, as trusting to their protection; while this opinion of the presence of their ancestors is a restraint that prevents their engaging in ill designs.

They despise and laugh at auguries, and the other vain and superstitious ways of divination, so much observed among other nations; but have great reverence for such miracles as cannot flow from any of the powers of nature, and look on them as effects and indications of the presence of the Supreme Being, of which they say many instances have occurred among them; and that sometimes their public prayers, which upon great and dangerous occasions they have solemnly put up to God, with assured confidence of being heard, have been answered in a miraculous manner. They think the contemplating God in His works, and the adoring Him for them, is a very acceptable piece of worship to Him.

There are many among them that upon a motive of religion neglect learning, and apply themselves to no sort of study; nor do they allow themselves any leisure time, but are perpetually employed, believing that by the good things that a man does he secures to himself that happiness that comes after death. Some of these visit the sick; others mend highways, cleanse ditches, repair bridges, or dig turf, gravel, or stone. Others fell and cleave timber, and bring wood, corn, and other necessaries, on carts, into their towns; nor do these only serve the public, but they serve even private men, more than the slaves themselves do: for if there is anywhere a rough, hard, and sordid piece of work to be done, from which many are frightened by the labour and loathsomeness of it, if not the despair of accomplishing it, they cheerfully, and of their own accord, take that to their share; and by that means, as they ease others very much, so they afflict themselves, and spend their whole life in hard labour: and yet they do not value themselves upon this, nor lessen other people's credit to raise their own; but by their stooping to such servile employments they are so far from being despised, that they are so much the more esteemed by the whole nation.

Of these there are two sorts: some live unmarried and chaste, and abstain from eating any sort of flesh; and thus weaning themselves from all the pleasures of the present life, which they account hurtful, they pursue, even by the hardest and painfullest methods possible, that blessedness which they hope for hereafter; and the nearer they approach to it, they are the more cheerful and earnest in their endeavours after it. Another sort of them is less willing to put themselves to much toil, and therefore prefer a married state to a single one; and as they do not deny themselves the pleasure of it, so they think the begetting of children is a debt which they owe to human nature, and to their country; nor do they avoid any pleasure that does not hinder labour; and therefore eat flesh so much the more willingly, as they find that by this means they are the more able to work: the Utopians look upon these as the wiser sect, but they esteem the others as the most holy. They would indeed laugh at any man who, from the principles of reason, would prefer an unmarried state to a married, or a life of labour to an easy life: but they reverence and admire such as do it from the motives of religion. There is nothing in which they are more cautious than in giving their opinion positively concerning any sort of religion. The men that lead those severe lives are called in the language of their country Brutheskas, which answers to those we call Religious Orders.

Their priests are men of eminent piety, and therefore they are but few, for there are only thirteen in every town, one for every temple; but when they go to war, seven of these go out with their forces, and seven others are chosen to supply their room in their absence; but these enter again upon their employments when they return; and those who served in their absence, attend upon the high priest, till vacancies fall by death; for there is one set over the rest. They are chosen by the people as the other magistrates are, by suffrages given in secret, for preventing of factions: and when they are chosen, they are consecrated by the college of priests.

The care of all sacred things, the worship of God, and an inspection into the manners of the people, are committed to them. It is a reproach to a man to be sent for by any of them, or for them to speak to him in secret, for that always gives some suspicion: all that is incumbent on them is only to exhort and admonish the people; for the power of correcting and punishing ill men belongs wholly to the Prince, and to the other magistrates: the severest thing that the priest does is the excluding those that are desperately wicked from joining in their worship: there is not any sort of punishment more dreaded by them than this, for as it loads them with infamy, so it fills them with secret horrors, such is their reverence to their religion; nor will their bodies be long exempted from their share of trouble; for if they do not very quickly satisfy the priests of the truth of their repentance, they are seized on by the Senate, and punished for their impiety.

The education of youth belongs to the priests, yet they do not take so much care of instructing them in letters, as in forming their minds and manners aright; they use all possible methods to infuse, very early, into the tender and flexible minds of children, such opinions as are both good in themselves and will be useful to their country, for when deep impressions of these things are made at that age, they follow men through

the whole course of their lives, and conduce much
to preserve the peace of the government, which suffers by nothing more than by vices that rise out of ill
opinions. The wives of their priests are the most extraordinary women of the whole country; sometimes the
women themselves are made priests, though that falls
out but seldom, nor are any but ancient widows chosen into that order.

None of the magistrates have greater honour paid
them than is paid the priests; and if they should happen to commit any crime, they would not be ques-
tioned for it; their punishment is left to God, and to
their own consciences; for they do not think it lawful to lay hands on any man, how wicked soever he
is, that has been in a peculiar manner dedicated to
God; nor do they find any great inconvenience in this,
both because they have so few priests, and because
these are chosen with much caution, so that it must
be a very unusual thing to find one who, merely out
of regard to his virtue, and for his being esteemed a
singularly good man, was raised up to so great a dignity, degenerate into corruption and vice; and if such
a thing should fall out, for man is a changeable creature, yet, there being few priests, and these having no
authority but what rises out of the respect that is paid
them, nothing of great consequence to the public can
proceed from the indemnity that the priests enjoy.

They have, indeed, very few of them, lest greater numbers sharing in the same honour might make the dignity of that order, which they esteem so highly, to sink in its reputation; they also think it difficult to find out many of such an exalted pitch of goodness as to be equal to that dignity, which demands the exercise of more than ordinary virtues. Nor are the priests in greater veneration among them than they are among their neighbouring nations, as you may imagine by that which I think gives occasion for it.

When the Utopians engage in battle, the priests who accompany them to the war, apparelled in their sacred vestments, kneel down during the action (in a place not far from the field), and, lifting up their hands to heaven, pray, first for peace, and then for victory to their own side, and particularly that it may be gained without the effusion of much blood on either side; and when the victory turns to their side, they run in among their own men to restrain their fury; and if any of their enemies see them or call to them, they are preserved by that means; and such as can come so near them as to touch their garments have not only their lives, but their fortunes secured to them; it is upon this account that all the nations round about consider them so much, and treat them with such reverence, that they have been often no less able to preserve their own people from the fury of their enemies than to save their enemies from their rage; for it has sometimes fallen out, that when their armies have been in disorder and forced to fly, so that their enemies were running upon the slaughter and spoil, the priests by interposing have separated them from one another, and stopped the effusion of more blood; so that, by their mediation, a peace has been concluded on very reasonable terms; nor is there any nation about them so fierce, cruel, or barbarous, as not to look upon their persons as sacred and inviolable.

The first and the last day of the month, and of the year, is a festival; they measure their months by the course of the moon, and their years by the course of the sun: the first days are called in their language the Cynemernes, and the last the Trapemernes, which answers in our language, to the festival that begins or ends the season.

They have magnificent temples, that are not only nobly built, but extremely spacious, which is the more necessary as they have so few of them; they are a little dark within, which proceeds not from any error in the architecture, but is done with design; for their priests think that too much light dissipates the thoughts, and that a more moderate degree of it both recollects the mind and raises devotion. Though there are many different forms of religion among them, yet all these, how various soever, agree in the main point, which is the worshipping the Divine Essence; and, therefore, there is nothing to be seen or heard in their temples in which the several persuasions among them may not agree; for every sect performs those rites that are peculiar to it in their private houses, nor is there anything in the public worship that contradicts the particular ways of those different sects. There are no images for God in their temples, so that every one may represent Him to his thoughts according to the way of his religion; nor do they call this one God by any other name but that of Mithras, which is the common name by which they all express the Divine Essence, whatsoever otherwise they think it to be; nor are there any prayers among them but such as every one of them may use without prejudice to his own opinion.

They meet in their temples on the evening of the festival that concludes a season, and not having yet broke their fast, they thank God for their good success during that year or month which is then at an end; and the next day, being that which begins the new season, they meet early in their temples, to pray for the happy progress of all their affairs during that period upon which they then enter. In the festival which concludes the period, before they go to the temple, both wives and children fall on their knees before their husbands or parents and confess everything in which they have either erred or failed in their duty, and beg pardon for it. Thus all little discontents in families are removed, that they may offer up their devotions with a pure and serene mind; for they hold it a great impiety to enter upon them with disturbed thoughts, or with a consciousness of their bearing hatred or anger in their hearts to any person whatsoever; and think that they should become liable to severe punishments if they presumed to offer sacrifices without cleansing their hearts, and reconciling all their differences. In the temples the two sexes are separated, the men go to the right hand, and the women to the left; and the males and females all place themselves before the head and master or mistress of the family to which they belong, so that those who have the government of them at home may see their deportment in public. And they intermingle them so, that the younger and the older may be set by one another; for if the younger sort were all set together, they would, perhaps, trifle away that time too much in which they ought to beget in themselves that religious dread of the Supreme Being which is the greatest and almost the only incitement to virtue.

They offer up no living creature in sacrifice, nor do they think it suitable to the Divine Being, from whose bounty it is that these creatures have derived their lives, to take pleasure in their deaths, or the offering up their blood. They burn incense and other sweet odours, and have a great number of wax lights during their worship, not out of any imagination that such oblations can add anything to the divine nature (which even prayers cannot do), but as it is a harmless and pure way of worshipping God; so they think those sweet savours and lights, together with some other ceremonies, by a secret and unaccountable virtue, elevate men's souls, and inflame them with greater energy and cheerfulness during the divine worship.

All the people appear in the temples in white garments; but the priest's vestments are parti-coloured, and both the work and colours are wonderful. They are made of no rich materials, for they are neither embroidered nor set with precious stones; but are composed of the plumes of several birds, laid together with so much art, and so neatly, that the true value of them is far beyond the costliest materials. They say, that in the ordering and placing those plumes some dark mysteries are represented, which pass down among their priests in a secret tradition concerning them; and that they are as hieroglyphics, putting them in mind of the blessing that they have received from God, and of their duties, both to Him and to their neighbours.

As soon as the priest appears in those ornaments, they all fall prostrate on the ground, with so much reverence and so deep a silence, that such as look on cannot but be struck with it, as if it were the effect of the appearance of a deity. After they have been for some time in this posture, they all stand up, upon a sign given by the priest, and sing hymns to the honour of God, some musical instruments playing all the while. These are quite of another form than those used among us; but, as many of them are much sweeter than ours, so others are made use of by us. Yet in one thing they very much exceed us: all their music, both vocal and instrumental, is adapted to imitate and express the passions, and is so happily suited to every occasion, that, whether the subject of the hymn be cheerful, or formed to soothe or trouble the mind, or to express grief or remorse, the music takes the impression of whatever is represented, affects and kindles the passions, and works the sentiments deep into the hearts of the hearers.

When this is done, both priests and people offer up very solemn prayers to God in a set form of words; and these are so composed, that whatsoever is pronounced by the whole assembly may be likewise applied by every man in particular to his own condition. In these they acknowledge God to be the author and governor of the world, and the fountain of all the good they receive, and therefore offer up to him their thanksgiving; and, in particular, bless him for His goodness in ordering it so, that they are born under the happiest government in the world, and are of a religion which they hope is the truest of all others; but, if they are mistaken, and if there is either a better government, or a religion more acceptable to God, they implore His goodness to let them know it, vowing that they resolve to follow him whithersoever he leads them; but if their government is the best, and their religion the truest, then they pray that He may fortify them in it, and bring all the world both to the same rules of life, and to the same opinions concerning Himself, unless, according to the unsearchableness of His mind, He is pleased with a variety of religions.

Then they pray that God may give them an easy passage at last to Himself, not presuming to set limits to Him, how early or late it should be; but, if it may be wished for without derogating from His supreme authority, they desire to be quickly delivered, and to be taken to Himself, though by the most terrible kind of death, rather than to be detained long from seeing Him by the most prosperous course of life. When this prayer is ended, they all fall down again upon the ground; and, after a little while, they rise up, go home to dinner, and spend the rest of the day in diversion or military exercises.

OF THEIR COMMONWEALTH

Thus have I described to you, as particularly as I could, the Constitution of that commonwealth, which I do not only think the best in the world, but indeed the only commonwealth that truly deserves that name.

In all other places it is visible that, while people talk of a commonwealth, every man only seeks his own wealth; but there, where no man has any property, all men zealously pursue the good of the public, and, indeed, it is no wonder to see men act so differently, for in other commonwealths every man knows that, unless he provides for himself, how flourishing soever the commonwealth may be, he must die of hunger, so that he sees the necessity of preferring his own concerns to the public; but in Utopia, where every man has a right to everything, they all know that if care is taken to keep the public stores full no private man can want anything; for among them there is no unequal distribution, so that no man is poor, none in necessity, and though no man has anything, yet they are all rich.

For what can make a man so rich as to lead a serene and cheerful life, free from anxieties; neither apprehending want himself, nor vexed with the endless complaints of his wife? He is not afraid of the misery of his children, nor is he contriving how to raise a portion for his daughters; but is secure in this, that both he and his wife, his children and grand-children, to as many generations as he can fancy, will all live both plentifully and happily; since, among them, there is no less care taken of those who were once engaged in labour, but grow afterwards unable to follow it, than there is, elsewhere, of these that continue still employed.

I would gladly hear any man compare the justice that is among them with that of all other nations; among whom, may I perish, if I see anything that looks either like justice or equity; for what justice is there in this: that a nobleman, a goldsmith, a banker, or any other man, that either does nothing at all, or, at best, is employed in things that are of no use to the public, should live in great luxury and splendour upon what is so ill acquired, and a mean man, a carter, a smith, or a ploughman, that works harder even than the beasts themselves, and is employed in labours so necessary, that no commonwealth could hold out a year without them, can only earn so poor a livelihood and must lead so miserable a life, that the condition of the beasts is much better than theirs? For as the beasts do not work so constantly, so they feed almost as well, and with more pleasure, and have no anxiety about what is to come, whilst these men are depressed by a barren and fruitless employment, and tormented with the apprehensions of want in their old age; since that which they get by their daily labour does but maintain them at present, and is consumed as fast as it comes in, there is no overplus left to lay up for old age.

Is not that government both unjust and ungrateful, that is so prodigal of its favours to those that are called gentlemen, or goldsmiths, or such others who are idle, or live either by flattery or by contriving the arts of vain pleasure, and, on the other hand, takes no care of those of a meaner sort, such as ploughmen, colliers, and smiths, without whom it could not subsist? But after the public has reaped all the advantage of their service, and they come to be oppressed with age, sickness, and want, all their labours and the good they have done is forgotten, and all the recompense given them is that they are left to die in great misery. The richer sort are often endeavouring to bring the hire of labourers lower, not only by their fraudulent practices, but by the laws which they procure to be made to that effect, so that though it is a thing most unjust in itself to give such small rewards to those who deserve so well of the public, yet they have given those hardships the name and colour of justice, by procuring laws to be made for regulating them.

Therefore I must say that, as I hope for mercy, I can have no other notion of all the other governments that I see or know, than that they are a conspiracy of the rich, who, on pretence of managing the public, only pursue their private ends, and devise all the ways and arts they can find out; first, that they may, without danger, preserve all that they have so ill-acquired, and then, that they may engage the poor to toil and labour for them at as low rates as possible, and oppress them as much as they please; and if they can but prevail to get these contrivances established by the show of public authority, which is considered as the representative of the whole people, then they are accounted laws; yet these wicked men, after they have, by a most insatiable covetousness, divided that among themselves with which all the rest might have been well supplied, are far from that happiness that is enjoyed among the Utopians; for the use as well as the desire of money being extinguished, much anxiety and great occasions of mischief is cut off with it, and who does not see that the frauds, thefts, robberies, quarrels, tumults, contentions, seditions, murders, treacheries, and witchcrafts, which are, indeed, rather punished than restrained by the severities of law, would all fall off, if money were not any more valued by the world? Men's fears, solicitudes, cares, labours, and watchings would all perish in the same moment with the value of money; even poverty itself, for the relief of which money seems most necessary, would fall. But, in order to the apprehending this aright, take one instance:–

Consider any year, that has been so unfruitful that many thousands have died of hunger; and yet if, at the end of that year, a survey was made of the granaries of all the rich men that have hoarded up the corn, it would be found that there was enough among them to have prevented all that consumption of men that perished in misery; and that, if it had been distributed among them, none would have felt the terrible effects of that scarcity: so easy a thing would it be to supply all the necessities of life, if that blessed thing called money, which is pretended to be invented for procuring them was not really the only thing that obstructed their being procured!

I do not doubt but rich men are sensible of this, and that they well know how much a greater happiness it is to want nothing necessary, than to abound in many superfluities; and to be rescued out of so much misery, than to abound with so much wealth: and I cannot think but the sense of every man's interest, added to the authority of Christ's commands, who, as He was infinitely wise, knew what was best, and was not less good in discovering it to us, would have drawn all the world over to the laws of the Utopians, if pride, that plague of human nature, that source of so much misery, did not hinder it; for this vice does not measure happiness so much by its own conveniences, as by the miseries of others; and would not be satisfied with being thought a goddess, if none were left that were miserable, over whom she might insult. Pride thinks its own happiness shines the brighter, by comparing it with the misfortunes of other persons; that by displaying its own wealth they may feel their poverty the more sensibly. This is that infernal serpent that creeps into the breasts of mortals, and possesses them too much to be easily drawn out; and, therefore, I am glad that the Utopians have fallen upon this form of government, in which I wish that all the world could be so wise as to imitate them; for they have, indeed, laid down such a scheme and foundation of policy, that as men live happily under it, so it is like to be of great continuance; for they having rooted out of the minds of their people all the seeds, both of ambition and faction, there is no danger of any commotions at home; which alone has been the ruin of many states that seemed otherwise to be well secured; but as long as they live in peace at home, and are governed by such good laws, the envy of all their neighbouring princes, who have often, though in vain, attempted their ruin, will never be able to put their state into any commotion or disorder".

———

When Raphael had thus made an end of speaking, though many things occurred to me, both concerning the manners and laws of that people, that seemed very absurd, as well in their way of making war, as in their notions of religion and divine matters – together with several other particulars, but chiefly what seemed the foundation of all the rest, their living in common, without the use of money, by which all nobility, magnificence, splendour, and majesty, which, according to the common opinion, are the true ornaments of a nation, would be quite taken away – yet since I perceived that Raphael was weary, and was not sure whether he could easily bear contradiction, remembering that he had taken notice of some, who seemed to think they were bound in honour to support the credit of their own wisdom, by finding out something to censure in all other men's inventions, besides their own, I only commended their Constitution, and the account he had given of it in general.

And so, taking him by the hand, I carried him to supper, and told him I would find out some other time for examining this subject more particularly, and for discoursing more copiously upon it. And, indeed, I shall be glad to embrace an opportunity of doing it. In the meanwhile, though it must be confessed that he is both a very learned man and a person who has obtained a great knowledge of the world, I cannot perfectly agree to everything he has related. However, there are many things in the commonwealth of Utopia that I rather wish, than hope, to see followed in our governments.

FINIS